NEW ROUTES FOR SOCIAL JUSTICE

About Policy Network

Policy Network is an international thinktank and research institute. Its network spans national borders across Europe and the wider world with the aim of promoting the best progressive thinking on the major social and economic challenges of the 21st century.

Our work is driven by a network of politicians, policymakers, business leaders, public service professionals, and academic researchers who work on long-term issues relating to public policy, political economy, social attitudes, governance and international affairs. This is complemented by the expertise and research excellence of Policy Network's international team.

A platform for research and ideas

- Promoting expert ideas and political analysis on the key economic, social and political challenges of our age.
- Disseminating research excellence and relevant knowledge to a wider public audience through interactive policy networks, including interdisciplinary and scholarly collaboration.
- Engaging and informing the public debate about the future of European and global progressive politics.

A network of leaders, policymakers and thinkers

- Building international policy communities comprising individuals and affiliate institutions.
- Providing meeting platforms where the politically active, and potential leaders of the future, can engage with each other across national borders and with the best thinkers who are sympathetic to their broad aims.
- Engaging in external collaboration with partners including higher education institutions, the private sector, thinktanks, charities, community organisations, and trade unions.
- Delivering an innovative events programme combining in-house seminars with large-scale public conferences designed to influence and contribute to key public debates.

www.policy-network.net

NEW ROUTES FOR SOCIAL JUSTICE

Empowering Individuals and Innovative Forms of Collective Action

Edited by
Claudia Chwalisz, Renaud Thillaye and Emma Kinloch

policy network

ROWMAN &
LITTLEFIELD
——INTERNATIONAL——

London • New York

Published by Rowman & Littlefield International Ltd
Unit A, Whitacre, 26-34 Stannary Street, London, SE11 4AB
www.rowmaninternational.com

Rowman & Littlefield International Ltd. is an affiliate of Rowman & Littlefield
4501 Forbes Boulevard, Suite 200, Lanham, Maryland 20706, USA
With additional offices in Boulder, New York, Toronto (Canada), and Plymouth (UK)
www.rowman.com

British Library Cataloguing in Publication Data

A catalogue record for this book is available from the British Library

ISBN: PB 978-1-78660-501-6
ISBN: eBook 978-1-78660-502-3

Library of Congress Cataloging-in-Publication Data
Library of Congress Control Number: 2017944925

∞ ™ The paper used in this publication meets the minimum requirements of
American National Standard for Information Sciences—Permanence of Paper for
Printed Library Materials, ANSI/NISO Z39.48-1992.

Printed in the United States of America

CONTENTS

ACKNOWLEDGEMENTS

This volume is the output of the fourth annual Policy Network and Foundation for European Progressive Studies (FEPS) Oxford conference that took place at St. Catherine's College, University of Oxford in July 2016. The conference explored a progressive reform programme for the institutional structure of society, the changing role of the state in the pursuit of social justice, and the evolving relationship between citizens and the state.

Most of the contributions in this volume are from speakers at this conference. We would like to thank all of those who presented in Oxford for helping shape our thinking – Geoff Mulgan, Nicolas Colin, Vicki Nash, Anthony Painter, Juha Leppanen, Selma Mahfouz, Andrew Harrop, Simon Parker, Mike Kenny, Georgia Gould, Alfred Gusenbauer, Ernst Stetter, Heleen de Boer, Anna Randle, Nick Pearce, Bart Vanhercke, Ben Page, Brando Benifei, Marte Gerhardsen and Robert Biedron.

We would also like to convey our thanks to Ania Skrzypek and Ernst Stetter from FEPS and Katherine Roberts from Policy Network who played a crucial role in facilitating the seminars. We are grateful to Ben Dilks and Charlie Cadywould for their help in editing the volume.

ABOUT THE CONTRIBUTORS

Ania Skrzypek is senior research fellow at the Foundation for European Progressive Studies (FEPS). She is an author of over 80 published papers and articles, available in English, French, German and Polish. Among her responsibilities at FEPS, she is in charge of the Next Left research programme, and co-ordinates FEPS Young Academics Network.

Ernst Stetter is the secretary general of the Foundation for European Progressive Studies (FEPS) since 2008. He is an economist and political scientist who comments regularly on EU affairs in the media, and is a visiting fellow at the University of Greenwich, London. In 2003 he received the French decoration of Chevalier de l'Ordre national du Mérite.

Claudia Chwalisz is a consultant at Populus and a Crook public service fellow at the Crick Centre, University of Sheffield. Previously a senior policy researcher at Policy Network, she is the author of *The Populist Signal: Why Politics and Democracy Need to Change* (2015) and *The People's Verdict: Adding Informed Citizen Voices to Public Decision-Making* (2017).

Renaud Thillaye is a manager at the business advisory firm Flint Global. He spent four years as an adviser to French local government leaders, before moving to the Bureau of European Policy

Advisors at the European Commission. Prior to joining Flint, he was deputy director and lead researcher and author on EU affairs at Policy Network.

Geoff Mulgan is chief executive of Nesta, and has been in post since 2011. Previously he was chief executive of the Young Foundation, director of the government's Strategy Unit and head of policy in the Prime Minister's office under Tony Blair. He has also been chief adviser to Gordon Brown, a lecturer in telecommunications, an investment executive, and a reporter on BBC television and radio.

Nicolas Colin is founder and partner of The Family, and a professor at Sciences Po and the University of Paris-Dauphine. He is the founder and former CEO of 1x1 connect, co-founder of Stand Alone Media, and was previously been commissioned by the French government to research the tax system and digital economy.

Florence Sutcliffe-Braithwaite is a historian of 20th-century Britain, and lectures at University College London. Her PhD examined political and popular ideas about class in England between 1969 and 2000. Other historical subjects she has an interest in include gender, sexuality and prostitution.

Hanno Burmester is a policy fellow at Das Progressive Zentrum where he researches the future of democracy. He works on organisational development in organisations across all sectors and sizes. In the past Hanno worked for a number of federal government institutions and as a freelance journalist, including for *NDR* and *die Taz.*

Georgia Gould is a Labour party councillor in the London Borough of Camden. Elected at the age of 24, she has led projects on youth unemployment, educational attainment and young people's civic engagement. Georgia is also the author of *Wasted: How Misunderstanding Young Britain Threatens Our Future.*

Tiina Likki is a senior advisor at the Behavioural Insights Team, leading its work on employment and welfare policy, as well as gender equality. Previously, she was an academic focusing on public attitudes towards the welfare state in Europe, and set up a think tank in Finland that introduced behavioural economics to Finnish public policy.

Anna Randle is director of public services at Collaborate CIC, joining in 2016 to develop its practice on citizen-focused services, helping public bodies square the challenge of radically reducing resources with services that value the insights and capacity, as well as the needs, of citizens. She previously worked as head of policy for the London Borough of Lambeth.

Charlie Cadywould is a researcher at Policy Network, leading its work on the future of the left. Prior to joining, he was a researcher at Demos, authoring numerous reports on social and economic policy, as well as various analyses of public opinion and voting behaviour. He holds a BA in social and political sciences from the University of Cambridge and an MSc in public policy from University College London.

Andrew Harrop has been general secretary of the Fabian Society since 2011, overseeing its research on economic and social policy as well as the future of the Labour party. He was previously director of policy and public affairs for Age UK. He has been a Labour party activist since the age of 18 and was a parliamentary candidate in the 2005 general election.

Ben Page is chief executive of Ipsos MORI. A frequent writer and speaker on trends, leadership and performance management, he has directed hundreds of surveys examining consumer trends and citizen behaviour. Ben is also a fellow of the Academy of Social Sciences and serves on advisory groups at the Kings Fund, Institute for Public Policy Research and Social Market Foundation. He is also a trustee at the Centre for London and a commissioner on the Resolution Foundation's Intergenerational Commission.

Emma Kinloch is impact and engagement manager in the Policy Institute at King's College London. Her work is focused on bringing research and policymaking closer together. Previously, Emma worked at Policy Network covering various operational roles, and was stakeholder relations manager for the network.

PREFACE

Reclaiming ground in the debate on the future of the state and the EU: For an agenda of collective aspirations, empowerment and participation

Ania Skrzypek and Ernst Stetter

At the time of publication, the world is already a very different place to the one we found ourselves in at the 'New Routes to Social Justice' seminars, held in Oxford in July 2016. Indeed, immediately after the UK referendum on its EU membership – the result of which was met with dismay across Europe – few could predict what was about to unfold. Many hoped there would be a long delay before the infamous activation of article 50. Instead, at the time of writing, it is obvious that thinking about what the EU-27 might look like in just 2 years' time requires a great deal of imagination and speculation.

Barely a month after Britain took the decision to leave the European Union, there was a great deal of uncertainty surrounding how the UK's departure from the EU would unfold and the impact of the referendum result on the wider world. Although it would be imprudent to jump to doomsday scenarios such as the collapse of the EU, the problems that the referendum campaign exposed remain unsolved and are echoed in the debates in other European states. Important questions remain over the role and powers of the EU, its members and their citizenries in shaping the course of events.

The dilemma mobilises two opposing sides. The first is composed of those advocating a retreat to nation states. They argue that disentangling from international structures would promote sovereignty and empowerment. Their adversaries believe that the only path forward is a simultaneous strengthening of the nation state and the EU, which are mutually dependent in shaping Europe's trajectory. Consequently, the choice to accelerate or retreat from integration was at the core of the elections in Austria, in the Netherlands, in Bulgaria and in France – to name just the recent examples.

While this dichotomy has constituted the battle lines for electorates in these countries, the debates also seem to reflect a division of populism versus pragmatism. In this context, what has most obviously been ignored as an alternative is progressivism. This shows how relevant and urgent it is for the centre left to regroup and try to reclaim the debate on the future of the state, the EU, and the institutional architecture of global governance.

The task is not easy, as it is both about changing the terms of the political conversation and about revisiting some of the past strategies that perhaps ended in a different place than initially desired. Here the major issue is the narrative of the 1990s, when globalisation trends became recognised in mainstream political discourse and when it was broadly argued that, in times of greater interconnectedness, singular states *cannot do too much*. The underlying thought was to offer a tangible argument in favour of internationalism and closer cooperation. The collateral damage it brought was the feeling that states and ultimately their citizens had been disempowered. This has been exacerbated in recent years, when people saw the financial crisis of 2008 undermining their security – leading them to taking the position of: '*right, let's bring the power to where we can see it exercised and give it to those who are bold enough to say no*', as illusory as such a rejectionist agenda of retreat can be.

To that end, what came out as an inspiration from the Oxford debate was the proposition that, while the nature of this electorally successful *antithesis* is clear, progressives stand a chance of changing the trend if they provide a *new thesis* to battle it with. They must reimagine the state and the EU it belongs to, looking to embody the principles of smart (as opposed to nationalism-driven) sovereignty and engage in reassuring, empowering and participatory relations with its citizens.

These three themes for citizen relations represent specific, progressive policy proposals. The first – reassuring – imprints the idea of social justice across the debate on rights and standards. It would have to go beyond the well known rhetoric of the crush and crunch times, defining both the minimums, as well as – and here is the difference to what is mainly being debated now – aspirations. The second theme – empowering – reinstates the social deal in a new way, urging not so much a defense of welfare systems, but their reinvention so that they can be effective vehicles of social progress in modern societies. And finally the third – participatory – should explore ways to reengage citizens not only occasionally during elections, but in all aspects of the political process. Here a debate about the future of political actors is essential, with an emphasis on the ways political parties, including progressives, should function to serve and deliver.

The same defining criteria should apply to the relations between Europe and its citizens, and it is imperative that progressives insist that the debate on the future of the state is inseparable from deliberations on the future of the Union. The recent anniversary of the Treaty of Rome, and the launch of a reflection, which the European Commission has framed as a choice among five scenarios, is more of an institutional reminder of it. More pressing is the fact that the choice facing the EU is not only about the ways and frameworks within which the states and the Union's bodies interact with one another. It is rather, first and foremost, about the strategy to solve the distributional conflicts that have emerged among states and people – as far as labour, welfare and prosperity shares are concerned. In that context, a progressive concept of a smart, sovereign state must be a component of a new vision for a social Europe.

That is the clear message from the written contributions included in this volume and from the two days of excellent, high level debate that FEPS, Policy Network and Renner Institut held for the fifth time in Oxford in July 2016. We would like to thank all the authors and participants for an incredibly stimulating set of ideas, and to express our gratitude to our partners for their cooperation, which offered the platform for these inspiring thoughts to be conceived.

INTRODUCTION

A new approach to power

Renaud Thillaye and Claudia Chwalisz

Social democracy as a model for social and economic organisation was one of the most remarkable achievements of the 20th century. Yet today, it comes short of offering attractive and credible new ideas that address the challenges of contemporary societies. Even while growth and unemployment figures may seem relatively stable after the immediate post-crisis years, most European economies are still facing numerous structural issues: productivity is sluggish; millions of people struggle to get by; inequality remains a monumental challenge; the mismatch between social contribution and economic reward pervades; the current low-quality, standardised way of providing public services has failed, and social cohesion is unravelling. Traditional social democrats still insist on offering top-down economic solutions on behalf of the people, a model of doing politics that reflects a society of the pre-internet era.

SOCIAL DEMOCRACY, WHAT NEXT?

In search of an alternative, there seem to be two main options for progressives. The first is a move toward the centre in an attempt to capture the open, liberal, progressive space. The second is a leftwing turn, combining historic social democratic values and a renewed platform for the 21st century. For instance, in France we see these two routes exemplified by Emmanuel Macron and his movement *En Marche!* on the one hand and Benoît Hamon in his Socialist party presidential bid on the other. In the UK, the centrist space is rather bare, while Labour party leader Jeremy Corbyn is trying out the second route to disastrous effect.

Both examples, however, highlight that a third way, moderate approach, which implicitly defends the status quo, is not the route to electoral victory. Neither is a radical leftwing platform, which scares people off and polarises people instead of uniting them. Circumstances help and personalities also matter. Martin Schulz's momentum in Germany is partly owed to Merkel fatigue and his ability to connect to ordinary voters rather than through ideological renewal. But thus far there seems to be a limit to this approach. Despite his rise in the polls, there was no evidence of a 'Schulz effect' in the recent regional elections.

While policy proposals matter and big 'tax and spend' questions remain important ideological markers, the centre left has a tendency of reducing all issues and problems to the economy. It is a misjudged approach for two reasons. First, it is a failure to recognise that having a shared sense of culture, values, and a feeling of belonging in the local and national community extends beyond economic concerns. Second, it misses that many people no longer want a paternalistic state to do everything for them. There is a demand for more open, inclusive democratic structures which give ordinary people (as opposed to politicians) a more meaningful voice in public decision-making. The centre left has too long left the issues of identity to the right, and lately to the far right, in the name of cultural relativism. It simply has not done enough on the latter concern about political processes, maintaining a belief in centralised political control.

This volume focuses on the latter issue about the ways in which politics and democracy need to change. All contributors share a number of assumptions on the shifting nature of government and put forward fresh ideas, for centre-left parties to grab, on how politics is done, policy is made and public services are delivered. The recurring theme is different ways in which government and political parties can empower individuals to be active citizens.

LOW TRUST IN INSTITUTIONS AND DEMOCRACY

As OECD data shows, trust in government has stagnated in the last ten years at an average of 43 per cent in OECD countries.[1] Some countries like Germany, Switzerland, New Zealand and Ireland have strengthened their above average position, but many others, including the US, France, Italy and Spain have fallen behind. Eurobarometer data show that trust in the EU, in national governments and parliaments has steadily declined over the past 15 years. People have limited faith in political parties and in representative democracy's capacity to solve their problems. In the UK, polling in *The Populist Signal* finds that only 21 per cent of people feel like their voice counts in the decision taken by elected politicians, and 68 per cent feel like the system of governing Britain needs to change.

Behind the success of the 'take back control' slogan in the Brexit referendum, there are no easy, obvious answers. Governments and political parties must find ways of adding value to people's lives again, but they cannot afford being seen as something that is done to people. They have to strike a delicate balance between giving people choice and a say in decisions, while providing more adapted protections and a renewed sense of belonging. Solving this dilemma does not lead to either small or big government, but more targeted interventions and a flexible government pragmatically looking at the most efficient ways of delivering public goods and services.

SOCIAL AND DIGITAL REVOLUTIONS

Government, and organisations playing a role in public life more generally, have yet to fully adjust to two profound social and technological changes. First, society has become more individualistic. As education levels have risen, voters have also demanded higher quality, customised public services. People are less ready to accept decisions that affect their daily life without being consulted or, at least, informed through maximum transparency. They demand easy ways to express their preferences and to provide feedback. Going down this route does not necessarily mean transforming government into an aggregation of individual interests. Deliberative and evaluation processes based on transparent and fair rules have a key role to play.

Second, digitalisation both accelerates this trend and gives organisations tools to 'process' the 'wisdom of the crowd' more easily. On the one hand, digitalisation empowers individuals, who can reach out to millions through social media. Groups of connected individuals can also initiate public campaigns and launch large scale initiatives. On the other hand, government and organisations have also gained access to smarter and more efficient ways of interacting with the public. Big data gives them the opportunity to understand their customers. Interactive platforms, artificial intelligence (AI) and the internet of things facilitate the aggregation of preferences and feedbacks. Provided personal data is not misused, this new technological environment for better government and democracy offers immense opportunities.

OPPORTUNITIES FOR PROGRESSIVES

Like digital platforms, government, parties and organisations have to make the most of the connected 'multitude' (to use Nicolas Colin's expression in this volume). Regardless of ideological orientations, collecting and processing data has become essential to political organisations and governments. It is a precondition for understanding people's needs, targeting offers, calibrating services, tracking delivery, learning from mistakes. In the analyses that have followed Donald Trump's victorious campaign, the role played by the audience targeting platform Cambridge Analytica has shed crude light on the power of data. At the very least, progressives should not lag behind conservative and populist forces when it comes to using technological innovations.

However, the opportunistic use of data and technology is not an end in itself. It does not necessarily meet people's desire to participate in decisions and experience engagement. It does not guarantee that insights from behavioural science, ie the aspects of human psychology which cannot be fully captured by technology, are fully taken into account. It does not ensure good government in the face of the unknown and in the unexpected. Restoring trust in government requires designing a whole set of 'default settings' at all stages of the political and policy process. More ambitious and systemic innovation is required at three stages:

1. **Participatory decision-making**: The usual complaint of citizens and party members is that decisions are taken away from them and take place behind closed doors. People's desire to be involved and have a say vary to a large extent. Representative democracy, for all its imperfection, should still be considered as a practical response to time, place and knowledge constraints. Nonetheless, an educated and informed public legitimately demands to be consulted or to participate.

   A possible default setting for decision-makers should be to institutionalise forms of participatory or deliberative decision-making. This is of course not suitable in all policy areas and circumstances as executive government is expected to make swift choices, especially in an emergency or in reaction to unexpected events. However, pieces of legislation introducing structural changes, construction or development projects, ethical issues, and long-term budgetary arbitrations should be more systematically subject to meaningful public engagement or deliberation. Digital tools can help reach out to people and, sometimes, engage them directly online.

   Innovations need not be digital-only, however. Randomly selected mini-publics such as citizens' juries or citizens' panels have proven to be an effective way for governments to gain legitimacy and public support for important public decisions.[2] Thus far these methods seem to be most frequently used in Canada and Australia, where groups of randomly selected citizens have played key roles in determining decisions as varied as updating Ontario's housing legislation pertaining to condominiums, Melbourne's 10-year $5 billion (AUD) financial plan, the state of Victoria's 30-year infrastructure policy and Canada's Mental Health Action Plan. Around fifty such examples exist. They demonstrate that by bringing together a wide cross-section of society, giving them the time and the resources to understand an issue, weigh the trade-offs and propose recommendations, better public decisions are made. Such moves to decentralise power more directly to citizens and communities rather than just to formal institutions are becoming more and more common. The politicians and parties that seize the move in this direction most quickly have the most to gain.

2. **Evidence based policy design**: When it comes to designing new policies, or reviewing existing ones, ideological preferences should systematically be weighed against data and scientific evidence. Gathering data has become relatively easy thanks to general connectivity once a robust infrastructure and legal framework are in place. Impact assessments and stakeholder and expert consultations are already the norm in a number of liberal democracies. However, some countries lead while others lag behind. The recent backlash against experts shows that communicating evidence to the wider public, and explaining evidence based choices, represents a new frontier.

3. **Iterative implementation**: Politicians and policymakers need to develop an experimental mindset and learn to seek constant feedback. Similar to digital platforms launching new features or changing settings, government and public organisations should, as much as possible, consider political and policy initiatives as steps forward on a longer journey. This implies trying, failing, repairing constantly, in order to find the most efficient way to get to the final destination. Randomised controlled trials and experiments should take place whenever possible in the roll-out phase.

Furthermore, letting the private sector make the most of big data and propose solutions to public organisations is something which left-leaning forces should not shy away from, as long as regulation and scrutiny are carefully thought through. Proactively seeking feedback through user reviews and regular external evaluations is another way to keep people in the loop.

Best practices abound. In reality, governance innovations have taken place for decades since it became clear that top-down management, both in private and public organisations, failed to improve quality and cost efficiency. However, with the digital acceleration and given the declining trust in democratic institutions, this agenda has become a priority. Not purely for efficiency, but more importantly for improving democracy.

CAVEATS

This is not to say that the road to electoral success for progressives is to position themselves as *the* champions of innovation. What should remain a means to an end too often becomes technocratic, geeky language that fails to capture people's imagination and possibly confuses them. In other words, progressives will not win elections purely by offering participatory democracy, evidence based policy-making and experimentations. The leave campaign invited people to 'take back control', but it did not embarrass itself with workable or rational solutions. Instead, it pandered to people's prejudice against immigrants and brandished a vague concept of sovereignty against Brussels. As suggested above, the left should not forget that a shared sense of culture, values, and a feeling of common belonging correspond to an essential need. This calls for a strong discourse allowing for emotional connection.

Innovative forms of collective action and the need for physical and emotional encounters are not mutually exclusive, on the contrary. Seeking public input into policy design and policy evaluation creates social opportunities. As Georgia Gould stresses in this volume, dedicating time and space for discussion helps engage and remobilise young people. More generally, it matters that politicians practise what they preach and are seen as trying to act in good faith. While not making this the core of their platform at an election, they should base their action on the assumption that the public is educated, that data can help a long way, and they themselves have a lot to gain from an iterative approach.

Such an agenda is not an ideological roadmap. It can be picked up by the centre right and the centre left. However, it is decisively anti-populist, embedded in evidence, open to criticism. For the centre left in particular, it represents a move away from seeing the state as the solution to society's problems and from a centralised, top-down approach to public decision-making. It calls for a new, restrained attitude from politicians: they represent certain orientations and values, but they are ready to exercise power in a different way. This volume is therefore more a contribution to the centre left's toolbox and approach to power rather than its programmatic renewal. By failing to use new opportunities offered by technology and science to better understand and meet people's needs, progressive forces risk further falling into irrelevance.

NOTES

1. OECD, 2017. 'Trust and Public Policy: How Better Governance Can Help Rebuild Public Trust', OECD Public Governance Reviews. Available at: http://www.oecd.org/gov/trust-and-public-policy-9789264268920-en. htm
2. Claudia Chwalisz, 2017 (forthcoming). *The People's Verdict: Adding Informed Citizen Voices to Public Decision-Making*. Rowman & Littlefield/Policy Network.

TOO LATE FOR THERAPY?

Or, what is to be done about the relationship between citizens and states

Geoff Mulgan

A lot is known about what makes relationships work. There needs to be trust and mutual respect, a willingness to accept differences, and a good mix of support, care and communication. Healthy relationships need constant work, and often need periodic reinvention.

Very similar considerations apply to the relationship between states and citizens, which so often appear fraught and strained to the point of breaking. By any historical standard the quality of the relationship between most democratic states and their citizens is good. They are more open, supportive and honest than ever before. We can remove bad governments; we know much more about what they do; and the quality of the services they provide has contributed to the extraordinary and unprecedented improvements in life expectancy, risks of violent crime and education achieved over the last 40 years or so.

But many citizens and commentators feel the opposite. Indeed it often looks as if we have moved from one set of unhealthy relationships – based on excessive servility and deference – to another set of unhealthy relationships marked by seething resentment and distrust, without even pausing for breath along the way. At the extreme there is anger and contempt; a view that governments and politicians are only in it for themselves; and an oddly infantilised mixture of belief that governments should be able to fix any problem and fatalism that nothing they do can ever work. The net result has been to increase the political space for a populism of denunciation, and to shrink the space for practical policy.

So what is to be done? What might a healthier relationship look like? Is it too late for therapy? Here I suggest some answers.

We need to start by disaggregating the question. The relationship between citizens and states is not singular. We relate to states in many different ways: as voters, campaigners, service users, or quiet beneficiaries of the state's capacity to provide peace or a stable economy. One dimensional views, whether romantic or cynical, can be misleading. Survey evidence confirms the public's differentiated feelings, with usually much more trust in those parts of the state which are close at hand and interacted with directly rather than observed indirectly through the media.

Each of these very different kinds of interaction then needs to be attended to as a relationship. The managerial theories that had so much influence in the last decades of the 20th century too often lost sight of this. An overly instrumental view of government squeezed out the space for affect. It was sometimes useful to think in the language of outputs and outcomes. But for the public it mattered how these were achieved too, just as in personal relationships we do not just want a spouse who will deliver a pay cheque or clean the house well.

A few years ago I argued in a series of papers that we needed to think in terms of a 'relational state'. That meant addressing what kinds of relationship citizens actually wanted, which turn out to be quite varied.

The romantics tended to assume that the ideal relationship had to much more active. An idealised view on the left and in some strands of liberalism wanted citizens to spend much of their time engaged in the uplifting work of governance. But in some cases people wanted the opposite: a more impersonal, frictionless and automated relationship with the state (paying taxes, applying for licences), that would leave them more time to get on with their lives.

In other cases, however, they did want the state to be much more human and engaged (eg with doctors, local police or politicians themselves). Indeed for many public services there is no avoiding the fact that most of the labour needed to produce better health, or better education, has to be done by citizens themselves rather than by service providers. This is even more true in an era when health services are dominated by chronic rather than acute diseases, and when ever-more education is needed to prepare for life and work.

Ethnography, conversation and deep listening can help in disentangling what is appropriate. These have become a prominent theme for the hundreds of public innovation labs that have grown up in national, regional and local governments around the world (Nesta helps link a network of them, providing newsletters, training and regular gatherings). Well known ones include Mindlab in Denmark, SITRA in Finland, the Seoul Innovation Bureau in Korea and the Laboratorio del Governo in Chile.

A high proportion of these labs emphasise citizen experience, as well as new uses of technology and data. And many aim to restore public trust.

Most of their projects focus on the practicalities of service delivery: jobs, education, taxation or transport. Reformers have found many ways to improve these everyday relationships. Websites provide ways for the public to communicate back to hospitals or police forces, and often it turns out that they want to thank or congratulate as well as complain. Officials have had to learn more conversational, and human, ways of responding. Budgets have been reshaped to give more control to the public over how funds relevant to them are spent. Personal accounts have been experimented with in many countries, particularly for social care, and are now being developed in new directions by Singapore and France in relation to training.

Citizens have also become much more active in helping states to see. Citizen generated data provides the inputs on everything from floods (Peta Jakarta in Indonesia) to corruption (Ipaidabribe in India), air quality (from China to Spain) to health.

Some of the labs are also interested in rethinking democracy itself in a more active, relational way. That does not mean perpetual referendums, a democracy of Facebook likes and binary choices. These are neither very effective at delivering good decisions or at increasing public trust. Instead platforms like DCENT, which Nesta developed with a group of European partners, aim to encourage more deliberation and discussion. They make it easier for citizens to track issues, to propose ideas, to comment, and in some cases to vote. These – in use now in cities including Barcelona, Madrid and Helsinki – allow democracy to tap the collective intelligence of the people, as well as harvesting a wider range of ideas.

These platforms work at multiple scales. They succeed most easily at the very local scale of the neighbourhood, dealing with issues of daily life, the management of public spaces or transport. They can also become part of the conversation in a city, as with Madrid Decide, closely tied into the role of the mayor. At national levels the tools seem to work better for more specialist topics, tapping into expertise that lies well beyond the political system, and allowing for detailed debates about options. They are rather less well suited to issues which are highly controversial, or founded very much on values and morality.

Seoul's mayor Won-Soon Park has probably been the world's most effective innovator on the citizen relationship, describing the citizens, not him as the mayor; introducing a vast range of new approaches to community involvement; pioneering more open approaches to data; reforming welfare provision and urban infra- structures. The ear outside city hall which allows people to propose and comment, and then shows the results inside the building, the mayor's dashboard of data which is also available online, and his over 2 million social media followers, all symbolise this more open, porous approach to governance.

Such richer styles of democracy are helped if governments and political parties can be more explicit about goals and means, and constraints, and more open about data and evidence. We at Nesta advocated, and helped establish some of what are now ten 'what works' centres in the UK providing different fields with syntheses of the state of knowledge – from policing and healthcare to schools and the economy. The simple idea is that anyone working in a field – such as schooling or eldercare – should have access to the best available knowledge in the world about what policies and practices are effective. That knowledge will often be uncertain or contested. But it is no longer acceptable for politicians or practitioners to be unaware of what is known. The aim is to provide deeper transparency about the knowledge guiding government, as a way of encouraging not just better results but also more trust.

This movement towards embedding evidence now has momentum at a global level – helped by formal structures within government such as South Africa or the Philippines, by parliamentary committees in countries such as Germany and Kenya. It can create discomfort for both politicians and the public – telling politicians that their cherished programmes do not work very well, and telling the public that the things they care about, like smaller class sizes or more police on the streets, may have little effects on improving outcomes. But greater visibility for evidence provides a foundation for a more adult relationship between states and citizens. It is still entirely reasonable for politicians or electorates to ignore the evidence – and of course they know that the experts have often been wrong in the past. But it is not acceptable for them to be ignorant of the evidence.

The media play a decisive role here. Some do all they can to fuel distrust, to undermine confidence in decision-makers and to promote appealing but impractical solutions. Others act more like mediators and guides, helping each better understand the others viewpoints. That sounds like a long shot. But it is what the best media already do, and the spread of fact checking sites, media committed to reasoned analysis, and intelligent blogging provides a counterweight to other powerful trends which dumb down debate.

For politicians the key, as in any relationship, is authenticity. Leaders need to explain what is and is not possible. Denouncing bureaucrats may win votes in the short term. But too much careless rhetoric corrupts political discourse, leaving inevitably unachievable expectations, cycles of illusion and disillusion. An adult conversation is a precondition for a restored relationship of trust with highly educated publics (the opposite may be true in other situations). There are few things more pathetic than a political leader who feels that they can only follow the public.

The various shifts described above – including a bigger role for evidence, data and citizen engagement - sometimes look to be at war with the alternative strands of 'post-truth' politics, and that strange hybrid of journalism and populist politics that sees little virtue in consistency or accuracy. But an optimistic view would see these as the natural direction of travel for more knowledgeable societies, and the only options we have if we want to believe that it is not, after all, too late for therapy.

PUBLIC POLICY IN THE DIGITAL AGE

The state as a platform

Nicolas Colin

For the fifth time since the end of the 18th century, our economy is undergoing the consequences of a technological revolution. As documented by Carlota Perez in her *Technological Revolutions and Financial Capital*,[1] every such revolution leads us through two consecutive phases: the installation phase, in which new technology driven markets are up for grabs as entrepreneurs and investors experiment with unproven business models; and the deployment phase, in which a new mode of growth, discovered through many trial and error efforts (and bursting bubbles),[2] is finally imposed onto the economy, industry by industry, leading to a new 'techno-economic paradigm'. [3]

The fifth revolution[4] is best understood through the history of personal computing. Thanks to the microprocessor, invented by Intel engineers in 1971, personal computing went beyond a narrow circle of hobbyists to finally hit mass markets. From 1991 onwards, the demilitarisation of the internet made it possible to connect all computing devices on the planet, giving birth to powerful net-worked applications . . . and to the dotcom bubble of the 1990s. More recently, the financial crisis of 2008 has triggered a rapid acceleration in the transition from the old Fordist paradigm to the digital one.[5] Technology companies are bursting into every industry to better serve digital-savvy consumers and force a redistribution of power between incumbents and new entrants.

As software is 'eating the world',[6] many pillars of our economy are rendered obsolete. From copyright[7] to taxation[8] to labour law[9] to taxi regulation,[10] brutal wars are waged around legacy institutions that were designed for the 20th-century Fordist economy, not for the emerging 21st-century digital economy. Indeed before we take existing social and economic institutions for granted, we have to realise that most of them were set up less than a century ago to fit the characteristics of the booming Fordist economy – and that nothing suggests that those institutions will outlast the now failing paradigm that gave birth to them. Hence it is urgent to understand what the digital age is and to reconsider the shape and role of the state so as to make the digital economy more sustainable and inclusive.

***

The first radical change concerns the essential resource that makes it possible for our economy to grow. The Fordist economy was born thanks to the abundance of cheap oil, which led to the birth of the car industry, the improvement of mass production through assembly lines, and the building of many institutions that explain the rise of the middle class, among them collective bargaining,[11] labour law and the social state.[12] Oil made urban sprawl possible, as it was needed to drive from the workplace to suburban areas and to perform critical functions such as heating in suburban homes. Oil also played a key role in many industries' supply chains and contributed a great deal to lengthening trade routes. We all realised the importance of abundant, cheap oil when it suddenly became scarce and expensive following the consecutive oil shocks in the 1970s: the economy immediately went off the rails, entering a long and painful period of economic stagnation and mass unemployment.

For a time, microelectronics was the digital equivalent of oil. Driven by the famous 'Moore's law',[13] cheap microelectronic components made it possible to produce ever cheaper and smaller computing devices. But as Moore's law enters a phase of exhaustion, we can finally see that the digital economy's essential resource is not the computing devices provided to individuals so much as it is the individuals themselves. The reason why tech companies are so eager to serve us well, to lower their prices and to make our lives easier through ever more innovative products is because we provide them with more than money. As we use their applications on a daily basis, we provide these companies with data (searching on Google and Amazon), tangible assets (our cars on BlaBlaCar, our homes on Airbnb), even creativity and our propensity to share (on YouTube, Facebook and SnapChat). The reason why individuals have become so valuable for tech companies is that we, as a multitude,[14] possess powers that every organisation must learn to harness in order to prosper in the digital age. Like oil in the past, this power is abundant and cheap, and the growth of the digital economy is based on the premise that it will stay this way.

Changes are happening in many dimensions – which is exactly what a transition between two techno-economic paradigms is about. Infrastructures change: we still need roads and bridges, but other infrastructures, such as cloud computing platforms, GPS satellites[15] and the internet itself, have become more critical. Products change: fewer manufactured goods, more digital applications and entertaining experiences. Organisations change: not the rigid, pyramidal bureaucracies that used to thrive in the Fordist economy, but more agile and innovative stacked architectures that combine user communities, digital activities, and tangible assets within a constantly evolving business model.[16] The managerial culture changes, too:

	FORDIST ECONOMY	DIGITAL ECONOMY
ESSENTIAL RESOURCE	OIL	MULTITUDE
ESSENTIAL INFRASTRUCTURES	RAILROADS, ROADS, ENERGY NETWORKS, POSTAL SERVICES	INTERNET, GPS, CLOUD COMPUTING, OPEN SOURCE, CONNECTED DEVICES
PRODUCTION	MASS PRODUCTION OF STANDARDIZED PRODUCTS	EXCEPTIONAL EXPERIENCE AT A LARGE SCALE
DOMINANT LINK	FACTORIES (MIDDLE OF THE VALUE CHAIN)	APPLICATIONS (DOWN THE VALUE CHAIN)
KEY BUSINESS MODEL FEATURE	ECONOMIES OF SCALE	INCREASING RETURNS
ORGANIZATION	HIERARCHICAL AND OPTIMIZED	AGILE AND INNOVATIVE
STRATEGIC GOAL	RESILIENCE	GROWTH
END CUSTOMERS	MASS	MULTITUDE

instead of being obsessed by economies of scale, efficiency gains and standardisation, managers are now focused on providing an exceptional customised experience and generating increasing returns at scale.[17]

The most striking change lies in the relationship between organisations and individuals. In the Fordist economy, organisations saw individuals as a mass of passive agents 'parked at the end of (their) value chain and eager to consume standardised products without demanding a better experience.[18] In the digital economy, the consuming masses have turned into a multitude of connected users that are both a consumption force and the essential resource that makes technology companies thrive. As a result, the corporate social contract has radically changed: the main balance of power is no longer between the shareholders and the employees, with the executives as an arbiter and the buyers as passive spectators.[19] Instead the multitude has become the strongest and most active party in the economy, with significant consequences for both corporations and the state.

The evolution of industry-wide value chains illustrates how those radical changes are imposed onto established organisations. Digital technologies are present in many companies, including those which were born before the digital revolution. But so-called technology companies, which were founded and grew with full knowledge of the transition at work, do more than use technology: they model their business so as to make the most of this technology and take positions that enable them to create and capture the most value. As the digital transition goes forward, the dominant companies are not those which operate factories in the middle of the value chain anymore, but a new breed of companies that design applications down the value chain, gaining the trust of the multitude and sealing an alliance with it. Factories still exist and add value, but they do not command as large a slice of the total value added as they did in the Fordist economy. Indeed, all dominant technology companies are now operating consumer oriented applications, frequently used by hundreds of millions – if not billions – of individuals at a global scale. The most emblematic car industry will soon be less dominated by car manufacturers than it will be by the likes of Google, Uber and Tesla Motors, which create a direct and trusted relationship with their end users through well designed applications.

***

In the Fordist economy, the state was a bigger version of large corporations. All the key organisations of the time were pyramidal and hierarchical, heavily processed, moved by a giant bureaucracy that traded scale against quality and efficiency against innovation. Yes, the customer experience was mostly bad, but at least the products were affordable at a large scale. Fordist organisations, with their Taylorist rules, assembly lines, and routine office tasks, proved the best way to provide large consumer markets with an affordable good or service. The same was true for public services: the welfare state, public transport systems and education policy were all modelled after the Fordist way – mass production of a standardised product. One-size-fits-all was the price to pay for public services to be widely affordable, especially in the context of tax revolts and fiscal austerity that prevailed from the 1970s onward.

Some countries were blessed by a historical coincidence: the centralised nature of their political system made their government apparatus particularly able to succeed at providing affordable public services in the Fordist economy. France is a case in point:[20] a hyper-centralised country ruled by a large bureaucracy, it entered the 20th century strengthened by the organisational legacy of both the Ancien Régime and the French Revolution,[21] all reinforced by Napoleon's establishment of the modern French public administration, legal system, and prestigious engineering schools. Those national traits became critical assets when it came to catching up in the Fordist economy. The French became the best at operating affordable public services at a very large scale. Their social state worked better than those in countries such as the US and Britain. They were even the best at implementing a so-called industrial policy designed to help national champions catch up and conquer dominant positions at an international scale[22]. To achieve that kind of outcome, it was better to inherit a centralised and resilient state: a 'cathedral', as coined by Eric Raymond,[23] that seemed tailored to sustain Fordist economic growth.

Alas, what worked well yesterday hardly fits today's new techno-economic paradigm. All of a sudden, the state as designed for the Fordist economy is less relevant as the digital economy rewards agility and innovation more than command-and-control and stan-dardisation. The dominant type of organisation in the new paradigm does not resemble a cathedral anymore. Rather, as suggested by the precedents of dominant tech companies, it is best described as a *plat-form*, serving as both an infrastructure and a marketplace on which supply and demand are more easily matched thanks to constant data driven innovations.[24] Instead of sustaining economic growth, the state as a cathedral now blocks progress and inspires anger and frustration in citizens who now expect radically different kinds of public services.

Indeed, a key property of platforms is increasing returns, those 'mechanisms of positive feedback that operate to reinforce that which gains success or aggravate that which suffers loss'.[25] Thanks to powerful network effects, both direct and indirect, platforms are able to increase their added value for individual users as they grow larger. This critical feature enables them to renounce traditional trade-offs such as that between quality and scale: contrary to their Fordist predecessors, platform-like organisations do not need to standardise their products and degrade their quality as they grow larger. In fact we observe quite the opposite: the larger the platform, the better the quality and the more diverse the supply. The rise of platforms and their replacing the old, bureaucratic organisations that we used to deal with explains the rapid evolution of individual expectations. One-size-fits-all was tolerated at a time when quality and diversity had to be sacrificed for the sake of scale.[26] It is not tolerated anymore, especially in the minefield of public services and the social state, in a paradigm where the multitude grows accustomed to being well served by constantly innovating tech companies.[27]

***

Can the cathedral morph into a platform – that is, an infrastructure and a marketplace on which a multitude of suppliers seize state provided resources to design better public services for ever more demanding citizens?[28] The answer is not clear. The previous technological transition, that from the age of steel and electricity to the age of mass production and consumption, did not see the state morph into a cathedral to comply with the needs of the nascent Fordist economy. Rather, the state was *already* a cathedral – it simply became more relevant and powerful than ever thanks to a historical coincidence that rewarded the kind of organisation that it already was.

What is more, those who lead the state today are lagging behind when it comes to realising that a transition is occurring and understanding where it is leading us. Compared to constituencies such as corporate executives, union leaders, scholars, and the voters themselves, our elected officials and civil servants are frighteningly unaware of the new platform model and the importance for the state to adapt both its form and its tools to become relevant again in the digital age.

Because it lags so far behind, the state is now confronted with a legitimacy crisis, and the rise of extremists in every advanced democracy can be interpreted as the reaction to both the weakening of the Fordist institutions and our elite's failure to build new ones that would lead us into a more sustainable and inclusive digital economy.[29] The challenge is especially daunting for leftwing parties, as they are the ones who used to prosper by making promises as to the state's ability to redistribute wealth and serve its citizens through better and more universal public services.[30] If leftwing elected officials tackle the challenge of turning the state into a platform, perhaps the left will come out of its current crisis and lead us into a digital golden age. But if they do not rise to the occasion, not only will the state plunge further into its current political and economic crisis, probably taking the entire economy down with it, but the left in and of itself will become increasingly irrelevant in the eyes of its discouraged voters.

NOTES

1. Carlota Perez, 2003. *Technological Revolutions and Financial Capital: The Dynamics of Bubbles and Golden Ages* (Cheltenham: Edward Elgar Publishing).

2. William H. Janeway, 2012. *Doing Capitalism in the Innovation Economy: Markets, Speculation, and the State* (Cambridge: Cambridge University Press).

3. Carlota Perez, 2009. "Technological revolutions and techno-economic paradigms" (Working Papers in Technology Governance and Economic Dynamics no. 20, The Other Canon Foundation, Norway, Tallinn University of Technology, Tallinn), http://technologygovernance.eu/files/main/2009070708552121.pdf.

4. The four previous revolutions led to the late 18th century Industrial Revolution, the age of steam and railways, the age of steel and electricity, and the Fordist age of oil, automobile, and mass production. See Carlota Perez, *Technological Revolutions and Financial Capital.*

5. John B. Judis, 2011. "Doom: Our economic nightmare is just beginning", *The New Republic*, September 14, 2011, https://newrepublic.com/article/94963/economic-doom.

6. Marc Andreessen, 2011. "Why Software Is Eating the World", *The Wall Street Journal*, August 20, 2011, http://www.wsj.com/articles/SB10001424053111903480904576512250915629460.

7. William Patry, 2009. *Moral Panics and the Copyright Wars* (Oxford: Oxford University Press).

8. Pierre Collin and Nicolas Colin, 2013. "Taxation and the Digital Economy" (Task force report commissioned by the French Government), http://www.hldataprotection.com/files/2013/06/Taxation_Digital_Economy.pdf.

9. Sara Horowitz, 2014. "America, say goodbye to the Era of Big Work", *The Los Angeles Times*, August 25, 2014, http://www.latimes.com/opinion/op-ed/la-oe-horowitz-work-freelancers-20140826-story.html.

10. Tim O'Reilly, 2015. "Networks and the Nature of the Firm", *What's the Future of Work?*, August 14, 2015, https://medium.com/the-wtf-economy/networks-and-the-nature-of-the-firm-28790b6afdcc#.yetiy02f8.

11. Nelson Lichtenstein, 2003. *State of the Union: A Century of American Labor* (Princeton: Princeton University Press).

12. Colin Crouch, 2009. "Privatised Keynesianism: An Unacknowledged Policy Regime", *The British Journal of Politics & International Relations*, 11: 382–399.

13. Named after Gordon Moore, a co-founder of Intel, *"whose 1965 paper described a doubling every year in the number of components per integrated circuit, and projected this rate of growth would continue for at least another decade"*. In fact Moore's law has remained true until at least 1998. "Moore's law – Wikipedia." Accessed October 28, 2016, https://en.wikipedia.org/wiki/Moore%27s_law/.

14. Nicolas Colin and Henri Verdier, 2012. "The Economics of the Multitude", *ParisTech Review*, June 7, 2012, http://www.paristechreview.com/2012/06/07/economics-multitude/. See also Paolo Virno, 2004. *A Grammar of the Multitude: For an Analysis of Contemporary Forms of Life* (Cambridge, MA: The MIT Press).

15. Tim O'Reilly, 2009. "Gov 2.0: It's All About The Platform", *Techcrunch*, September 4, 2009, https://techcrunch.com/2009/09/04/gov-20-its-all-about-the-platform/.

16. Philip Evans, Patrick Forth, 2015. "Borges' Map: Navigating a World of Digital Disruption", *BCG Perspectives*, http://digitaldisrupt.bcgperspectives.com/.

17. W. Brian Arthur, 1996. "Increasing Returns and the New World of Business", *Harvard Business Review*, July-August, https://hbr.org/1996/07/increasing-returns-and-the-new-world-of-business.

18. Nilofer Merchant, 2013. "We need a new language for the collaborative age", *Wired UK*, March 8, 2013, http://www.wired.co.uk/article/we-need-a-new-language-for-the-collaborative-age.

19. Nicolas Colin, 2016. "A New Corporate Contract for the Digital Age", *The 8th Global Drucker Forum Blog*, October 19, 2016, https://www.druckerforum.org/blog/?p=1364.

20. Philip Nord, 2010. *France's New Deal: From the Thirties to the Postwar Era* (Princeton: Princeton University Press).

21. Alexis de Tocqueville, 2008. *The Ancien Régime and the Revolution* (New York City: Penguin Classics).

22. William H. Janeway, 2013. "The Two Innovation Economies", *Project Syndicate*, April 10, 2013, https://www.project-syndicate.org/commentary/china-and-the-frontiers-of-innovation-by-william-janeway.

23. Eric S. Raymond, 2001. *The Cathedral and the Bazaar: Musings on Linux and Open Source by an Accidental Revolutionary* (Cambridge, MA: O'Reilly Media).

24. Marshall W. Van Alstyne, Geoffrey G. Parker and Sangeet Paul Choudary, 2016. *Platform Revolution: How Networked Markets Are Transforming the Economy--And How to Make Them Work for You* (New York City : W. W. Norton & Company, 2016). See also Marshall W. Van Alstyne, Geoffrey G. Parker and Sangeet Paul Choudary, "Pipelines, Platforms, and the New Rules of Strategy", *Harvard Business Review*, https://hbr. org/2016/04/pipelines-platforms-and-the-new-rules-of-strategy.

25. W. Brian Arthur, "Increasing Returns and the New World of Business".

26. Babak Nivi, 2013. "The Entrepreneurial Age", *Venture Hacks*, February 25, 2013, http://venturehacks.com/articles/the-entrepreneurial-age .

27. Matt Bai, 2011. "What Steve Jobs Understood That Our Politicians Don't", *The New York Times*, October 6, 2011, http://thecaucus.blogs.nytimes. com/2011/10/06/what-steve-jobs-understood-that-our-politicians-dont.

28. Tim O'Reilly, 2013. "Government as a Platform", in *Open Government*, ed. Tim O'Reilly (Cambridge: O'Reilly Chimera), http://chimera. labs.oreilly.com/books/1234000000774/ch02.html.

29. Nicolas Colin, 2016. "Brexit: Doom, or Europe's Polanyi Moment?", *The Family Papers*, June 27, 2016, https://salon.thefamily.co/ brexit-doom-or-europes-polanyi-moment-3e97269e6b67.

30. Franklin Foer, 2013. "Obamacare's Threat to Liberalism", *The New Republic*, November 25, 2013, https://newrepublic.com/article/115695/ obamacare-failure-threat-liberalism.

PARTY POLICY AND SERVICE DELIVERY

Process vs outcome

Florence Sutcliffe-Braithwaite

A division has opened up within the left in recent years between those who believe the process of policymaking and delivery of services should be changed, and those who argue – tacitly or implicitly – that the left should focus on *outcomes*, not processes. But the social and cultural changes that have taken place in British society since c. 1945 mean that while a focus on outcomes once made sense for the left, we need to change our approach. Political *processes* – engaging individuals and communities in shaping policy and service delivery – should now be given significant weight alongside the left's traditional concern with changing outcomes.

This division within the left mirrors, but does not map precisely onto, older debates. In the late 19th and early 20th centuries, there were two broad tendencies among socialists in Britain. Some wanted socialism to amount to a whole new way of life; to rethink everything from economic production to relationships between men and women. Others thought the priority for socialist or social democratic politics was amassing electoral coalitions large enough to take power (at local and national level) and effect gradual change to improve the lives of the working classes.

The latter approach has given us huge successes since the early 20th century: advances in workers' rights and wages, in social security, in health, housing, and education, and in tackling poverty and inequality. However, social and cultural changes that have occurred since c. 1945 mean people are now less comfortable with paternalistic politics: with politics from above in which people are, or feel, relatively powerless. The Brexit campaign and referendum result show how importance it is to recognise this. The time is therefore ripe for reassessing the parameters of change that leftwing politics wishes to achieve. Changing how policy is made and how service delivery is organised offers an opportunity to expand the remit of social democratic politics. In the rest of this chapter, I examine some of the most significant social and cultural changes of the postwar period, and then suggest the political approaches they might point towards.

CULTURAL AND SOCIAL CHANGE SINCE C. 1945

Britain's class landscape has been transformed since the 1950s in many and complex ways. This is not to deny that Britain remains a nation with vast, structured inequalities. But things have changed. The 1950s was the (brief) high point of class based voting in Britain. As Shirley Williams reflected, "Elections in the 1950s and 1960s were dominated by class. I could walk up the garden path and guess nine times out of ten how the people in the house would vote. Most of those in council houses would be Labour voters".[1] This soon began to break down, though, and the 1970s was labelled the 'decade of dealignment'. Now class is less useful as a predictor of voting; ideas and values have, conversely, risen in importance as determinants of voting.[2]

What class means in people's lives has changed in broader ways, too. Across the postwar period, overall inequality fell to a low point in the mid-1970s, before soaring under Thatcher. Over the same period, white collar jobs grew as a proportion of the total workforce; but some have argued that a growing proportion of these jobs have been 'proletarianised'.[3] Being a white collar worker may not mean what it once did. Simultaneously, the welfare state and mass prosperity and consumerism have radically transformed lifestyles. When one woman (a miner's daughter, born in 1937) was interviewed for the Millennium Memory Bank, a major BBC oral history project in 1999, she commented that the "boundaries have moved or been moved . . . my children and grandchildren live in a completely different lifestyle from the one I was brought up in." The interviewer asked whether she would say they were 'more middle class', and Dyke answered,

> "By some definitions . . . middle class now no longer means what it meant when I was a child . . . [then it] had the notion of bay windowed . . . bathroomed, wall-to-wall carpeting . . . semi-professional background . . . that's pretty much the norm these days wherever there are people who are working."[4]

The result of these complex changes in the economy, wages, the welfare state and consumerism is that the class structure has grown more fragmentary. One recent sociological analysis found that there were at least seven distinct classes in Britain.[5] Perhaps unsurprisingly, then, individuals' understanding of their 'class identity' is often, nowadays, complex and fraught. Many people have a strong attachment to authenticity and to their family roots; but this often goes along with a scepticism of class categories that are seen as crude labels that deny individuality. In the Millennium Memory Bank interviews, many interviewees made comments along the lines that the 'vast majority' of people were becoming 'classless',[6] or that there was now 'a wide range of working middle class people'.[7] Elites who are seen as not having to 'play by the rules', however, are often excluded from this 'ordinary' majority.

Gender roles and class cultures have always been mutually constitutive, and revolutions in gender roles in the postwar period have, therefore, contributed further to unsettling stereotypical 'class' images. The immediate postwar decades saw an unprecedented increase in married women working outside the home; the post-1969 feminist movement and LGBT activism challenged traditional gender roles and traditional sexual mores in even more radical ways, making Britain a far more diverse place by the early 2000s. One commentator wrote as early as 1989 that 'gender convergence' was the critical missing link in understanding changes in class consciousness in the postwar period.[8] Recent historical research shows that ideologies of marriage, and men's and women's roles as fathers and mothers – some of the most central experiences of most individuals' lives – became far more 'classless' in the postwar period.[9] And how parents and children related to each other changed, too; in the 'affluent society' of postwar Britain, more and more parents wanted their children to have more opportunities, more freedom, more fun, than they had had as young people.[10] Broadening aspirations were passed down through families.

There were further important shifts in how people approached questions of sex, gender, and family, across the latter half of the 20th century. In the 1940s, for many, marriage was still a sacred institution. Duty and tradition were highly important, and divorce stigmatised. By the 21st century, not only was divorce far more common, but the considerations people would take into account when deciding when to end a marriage were different: duty and tradition had been downgraded; religious teaching is now a consideration for only a minority of people; the wellbeing of children, and the personal fulfilment of each of the partners in the marriage are now seen as the vital questions. Thus changes relating to gender and sexuality were linked to broader shifts in emotional cultures. 'Character', self-control and strength became less important in codes of masculinity.[11] Instead, openness, emotion and self-expression became more valued. And across society, so did individual self-actualisation and fulfilment.

When it comes to race, too, Britain is now a far more diverse society than it was in 1945; but we are also a self-consciously multicultural society. Cultural difference and exchange are widely celebrated as enriching our society. Few in Britain have claimed that the assimilationist model followed by states like France should apply here. And, as with gender and sexuality, race has been the subject of waves of 'identity politics' activism and organising since the late 1960s. The

very basis of these identity politics movements has been the asser-
tion that individuals should organise to fight their own oppression,
not wait for elites to fight it for them. As the name implies, these
movements put individual identity centre stage. These social and
cultural changes, then, have made the class landscape of Britain more
complex and fragmented; and in their wake, people value individual
expression, identity, openness, choice and fulfilment more.

Many theorists have seen these various social and cultural changes
as parts of a larger shift, variously called the rise of individualism,
the decline of deference, or the rise of postmaterialist values. In
the 1990s, Anthony Giddens argued that what he called the 'new
individualism' did not simply mean 'the "me" generation', but
was a whole new orientation to life focused on self-fashioning and
choice. It was the result of 'the retreat of tradition and custom from
our lives'.[12] The 'new individualism' was, thus, entirely compatible
with a desire for good public services and a less unequal society.
And, in fact, it often went along with strong ethical attachments, frequently to what Ronald Inglehart called 'postmaterialist values': the
environment, peace, antiracism, etc Inglehart first sketched out his
theory of 'postmaterialist values' in the 1970s, suggesting that mass
affluence and greater security than ever before – with welfare states
and high employment levels – had allowed more and more people
to value abstract, ethical goods in politics, alongside questions of
material distribution.[13] In this reading, Attlee had helped foster the
growth of 'postmaterialist values'. A profoundly paternalistic postwar settlement paved the way for the decline of deference to government, elites and experts. The decline of deference to politicians is
one factor in the rise of 'antipolitical' sentiments,[14] and in populist
insurrections and the EU referendum result. The rise of individualism and postmaterialist politics has played a role in the rise of small
parties like the Greens and UKIP.

Social and cultural change, then, has made British society more
fragmented; people now value control and choice more, are sceptical
of the power of elites or the wisdom of experts. These are not
changes the left can – or should – want to reverse. We cannot go

back to paternalism. The challenge is to rethink politics to make it chime with these values.

MAKING AND DELIVERING POLICY IN AN INDIVIDUALISTIC SOCIETY

These social and cultural changes, particularly the fragmentation of society and the decline of deference, have important implications for how people want to interact with government and how important the means, as well as the ends, are. They mean that the left should be looking to devolution, localism, and democratic innovations as routes through which people can be empowered and engaged in making policy and shaping the delivery of services.

Anger about policymaking and public services being distant and unaccountable is not new. By the late 1960s and 1970s, community activists and New Left thinkers were critiquing the bureaucratic, remote social democratic state. Many working people felt the same; Alan Johnson wrote in his memoir of the education system in the 1970s:

> "At that time, schools were still closed institutions, as they had been in my schooldays. Parental interest was discouraged, performance standards were opaque and achievements were not measurable by any meaningful comparison. Schools were largely immune from outside scrutiny."[15]

Thatcher and Major tried to address these frustrations by framing the users of public services as 'consumers' – hence Major's famous 'cones hotlines'. This was a route New Labour partly continued down. But this approach attenuates public engagement with politics and public services. Participating actively as citizens – ie as individuals but with an eye also to collective identities and the good of the community – offers a more meaningful way forward.

Many voices on the left have argued in recent years that democratic innovations, localism and devolution provide such a route. Democratic innovations provide ways to deepen the 'thin' experience of democracy that citizens get from merely voting in occasional elections. Deliberative democracy offers a way to engage citizens in shaping important policy decisions in their area, region or nation; where politicians are committed to the process it has led to progressive and egalitarian policies, greater citizen engagement and more public confidence in politics.[16] The New Economics Foundation's New Deal for Coastal Communitites shows the potential of developing green solutions to regenerate communities from the ground up.[17] Local governments around the world are already showing how, in different ways, they can use their power, influence, and commissioning budgets to localise and democratise economies and public services.[18]

Democratising workplaces, by extension, should also interest the left, and here, too, there are powerful examples which suggest that cooperative models and worker participation and control in the direction of industry can be popular *and* lead to economically sustainable and successful businesses.[19] And giving the users of public services more control over how those services are delivered can, if done properly, enhance the control they have over their daily lives, as well as, in some cases, being more efficient.

When Jeremy Corbyn was elected as Labour leader, he quickly announced that 'the democratisation of public life from the ground up' would be a key aim of any government he led. It is striking that both Tony Blair and Gordon Brown also promised, on coming to power, to give power to the people and extend and deepen democracy.[20] There was much important constitutional reform under Blair, and some under Brown, but the architects of New Labour were also attracted to the centralisation of power – understandably, for it enabled them to deliver major policies like the minimum wage, tax credits and Sure Start centres, and thus drive significant change in British society.

David Cameron and George Osborne's embrace of localism was often cover for slashing poor local authorities' budgets quicker than rich ones, and devolving responsibility and blame for cuts. This has made many on the left sceptical of such an agenda. These fears dovetail with longstanding anxieties that localism and democratic innovations might lead to unpopular 'postcode lotteries' and inconsistencies in service provision, entrenching inequality and undermining public confidence in the state and in politics. But inequality is already high and faith in politics low. We should, therefore, give real thought to the potential for localism and democratic innovation to reshape our politics and society.

Emily Robinson has identified four obstacles in the way of such an agenda: the attractions to any party in government of the strong executive power the British constitution offers them, Labour's ingrained constitutional conservatism, its lack of a theory of the state, and, finally, the sense that constitutional matters are not a priority for social democrats. As Robinson says, meaningful change requires 'resolution, persistence and – above all – a coherent strategy and reason for doing so' (Robinson 2016, 115).[21] An important part of the reason for doing so is supplied by an examination of the social and cultural changes that have swept Britain since 1945. The more fragmented and diverse, less deferential, more individualistic society that has developed since the second world war means that changing the process by which we do politics is not merely a utopian vision but vital to restoring public faith in politics.

NOTES

1. Shirley Williams, 2009. *Climbing the bookshelves: The autobiography of Shirley Williams*. London: Virago.

2. Bo Särlvik and Ivor Crewe, 1983. *Decade of dealignment: The Conservative victory of 1979 and electoral trends in the 1970s*. Cambridge: Cambridge University Press.

3. Rosemary Crompton and Gareth August Jones. 1984. *White-collar proletariat: Deskilling and gender in clerical work*. London: Macmillan.

4. Mel Dyke, Millennium Memory Bank (MMB) C900/14558 C1, British Library National Sound Archive.

5. Mike Savage, Fiona Devine, Niall Cunningham, Mark Taylor, Yaojun Li, Johs. Hjellbrekke, Brigitte Le Roux, Sam Friedman and Andrew Miles, 2013. "A new model of social class: findings from the BBC's British Class Survey experiment." *Sociology* no. 47:219–250. doi: 10.1177/0038038513481128.

6. Dominic Hardy, MMB C900/17558 C1.

7. Kuli Padan, MMB C900/17597 C1.

8. Nicky Hart, 1989. "Gender and the Rise and Fall of Class Politics." *New Left Review* no. 175 19–47.

9. Angela Davis, 2012. *Modern motherhood: Women and family in England, c. 1945–2000*; Laura King, 2015. *Family men: Fatherhood and masculinity in Britain, 1914–1960*. Oxford: Oxford University Press.

10. Selina Todd, and Hilary Young, 2012. "Baby-boomers to 'Beanstalkers': Making the modern teenager in post-war Britain." *Cultural and Social History* no. 9 (3):451–467. doi: 10.2752/147800412X13347542916747.

11. Martin Francis, 2002. "Tears, Tantrums, and Bared Teeth: The Emotional Economy of Three Conservative Prime Ministers, 1951–1963." *Journal of British Studies* no. 41 (3):354–387. doi: 10.1086/341153; Mathew Thomson, 2006. *Psychological subjects: Identity, culture, and health in twentieth-century Britain*. Oxford: Oxford University Press.

12. Anthony Giddens, 1998. *The Third Way: The renewal of social democracy*. Cambridge: Polity Presss

13. Ronald Inglehart, 1997. *Modernization and postmodernization: Cultural, economic, and political change in 43 societies*. Princeton, N.J.: Princeton University Press.

14. Gerry Stoker, Jonathan Moss, Nick Clarke and Will Jennings. 2016. "Anti-Politics and the left." *Renewal* no. 24 (2):9–18.

15. Alan Johnson, 2015. *Please, Mister Postman*. London: Corgi.

16. Claudia Chwalisz, 2016. *The populist signal: Why politics and democracy need to change*. London: Policy Network; Oliver Ecscobar, 2016. "Beyond anti-politics through democratic innovation." *Renewal* no. 24 (2):21–24.

17. Fernanda Balata, 2016. "Shaping a new deal for coastal communities." *Renewal* no. 24 (2):79–83.

18. Marjorie Kelly, Sarah McKinley and Violetta Duncan. 2016. "Community Wealth Building: America's Emerging Assetbased Approach to City Economic Development." *Renewal* no. 24 (2):51–68; Matthew Brown and Martin O'Neill, 2016. "The Road to Socialism is the A59: The Preston Model." *Renewal* no. 24 (2):69–78.

19. Thomas Ferretti, 2015. "Mondragon in Five Points." *Renewal* no. 23; Joe Guinan, 2015. "Bring Back the Institute for Workers' Control." *Renewal* no. 23.

20. Emily Robinson, 2016. "Citizenship and the constitution." In *Rebuilding social democracy*, edited by Kevin Hickson, 111–126. London: Policy Press.

21. Robinson, "Citizenship and the constitution." 111–126.

HOW MAYBE NOT TO DIE

Ideas for innovating traditional parties

Hanno Burmester

Democracy is existentially threatened. Mistrust of democratic institutions has trickled down into the very centre of our societies. We see steadily declining confidence in government, parliaments, and parties. Indeed, public discontent can be seen far beyond typical 'protest voters' for several years now. People are afraid of losing social and economic status, being faced with complex societal, economic and political challenges that can neither be easily explained nor easily solved (climate change, globalization, the digital economy, war and migration, etc).

The political sphere is faced with an increasing number of 'wicked problems', characterised by complexity, a high degree of insecurity, and a conflict of values and norms that cannot be solved by political compromise. There seems to be a clash of paradigms: machinist thinking against systems thinking, Fordist against digital organisations, internationalism against nationalism, materialism against postmaterialism, etc. The political sphere seems paralysed, not only because of a lack of orientation, but also because of the increasing organisational incapability of meeting the challenges we face today. As a consequence, the number of votes for populist forces rises, and political grassroots movements of all sorts become more popular, while established democratic organisations erode.

For many citizens, political solution strategies are barely com-
prehensible. Due to the high degree of complexity, political actors
and institutions – elected to solve problems – more and more often
seem incapable of acting in any meaningful way. At the same time,
the core ideas and principles of democracy still enjoy high approval.

It is important to note that considerable parts of public discontent
are directed against the manner in which policies are made, not
against the results of political processes.[1] The need to reform democracy thus is triggered not only by public distrust and alienation, but
also by discontent with the organisational structures and processes
that were designed decades ago. Indeed, few democratic organisations seem to fit our times. While their core purpose is broadly
accepted, their organisations' paradigms are outdated and severely
overstretched at the same time.

In a year-long project, we looked at traditional German party
organisations, and how they can innovate in order to minimise the
gap between societal expectations and intra-organisational culture,
structure, and process.[2] In their essence, parties work the way they
did in the 1950s. Like large corporations, their structure hinders
successful innovation instead of promoting it. This not only limits
their capacity to recruit high skilled talent, but also to develop gold
standard programmatic ideas from the bottom up.

While constantly asking their voters to change, most traditional
parties fail to do exactly this. At the same time, our societies need
political parties, arguably more than ever. No other institution is able
to master the complexities of our democratic systems with such a
depth of knowledge and experience. No other institution is willing
to focus its activities on the common interest, instead of focussing
on special interest like NGOs do. Also, no other institution provides
comparable potential for intra-societal dialogue and understanding
– something we need more than ever in our increasingly disparate
societies.

Like all other big organisations, political parties are directly
exposed to societal transformation: demographic change, new
work habits and environments, and digitalisation of work and

communication. Hence, their change is not an end in itself. New organisational structures are the foundation for a political party's sustained legitimacy as one of the key drivers of change in society. Adapting to the changes may seem like a giant challenge, but is the only way for parties to maintain long term success and political effectiveness as an organisation.

For years now, political insiders have been saying that it is close to impossible to substantially innovate party organisations. I think this is nothing but a blatant self-excuse. Human-designed structures can be changed by humans. But dedicated leadership is needed to reform any organization with decade-old cultures and structures. Of course, it takes more than one party leader to initiate meaningful change. It takes the entire top leadership, and allies all over the party hierarchies in order to get things done that are more than just hesitant, incremental steps. And, even more importantly, outside perspectives are necessary in order to break up the routines of an increasingly homogenous membership.

Like most organisations I work with, parties discriminate in favour of those who obstruct change. People who want to initiate a project or change something in their organisational realm must pitch and defend their ideas – they are the ones who are supposed to deliver the evidence that innovation would be better than the status quo. This mostly means that innovation gets shot down before really unfolding its potential. In today's meeting culture, we tend to corrode and destruct instead of improving and developing ownership for new thoughts and ideas.

Why not change this setting and turn it upside down – especially in parties, which rely on motivated members who enjoy a high degree of self-efficacy? People with new ideas should be empowered instead of discouraged. Organisational models like Holacracy offer ideas for how this can be done: by changing the default settings for decisions (and thus meetings), and by systematically implementing structures that incentivise proactive change on all levels.[3] The substantive game changer is: whoever wants to obstruct innovation needs straight evidence in order to use a veto. If there is no such evidence, the person who wants to change can go ahead and just do so (of course, evaluation and improvement of any new measure follow). This radically shifts power from the unwilling to those who want to innovate.

I highly doubt that any of the established parties will be willing to seriously consider such a step in the near future. It will take a bigger number of new, agile competitors – parties that from the beginning of their existence use innovative organizational paradigms, something like the Spanish Podemos or the Danish Alternativet – in order to make the traditional agents not only self-reflect the way they work, but also act in new ways. Which, basically, means choosing a customer centred perspective instead of continuously prioritising the perspective of those who deeply enjoy their decade-long drive on a sinking ship, unwilling to even seriously consider changing course.

Until then, more incremental changes are needed. In this article, I want to introduce five steps that are doable even with today's limitations:

1. Get to know your volunteers better
In order to design offers that match today's needs, parties need to gather more knowledge and data about their members and potential volunteers. Strategic development of the volunteer base and, therefore, of the entire organisation is hardly possible if there is a lack of insight into the members' political interests, time budgets, competences, and available qualifications.

- **Systematically learn about volunteers:** Political parties should collect more information (and thus data) about their members and sympathisers, in order to adjust offers to their actual needs and wishes.
- **Introduce parallel membership models:** Activists should be able to pick their preferred way of working when entering party membership. One way to open up parallel pathways could be the design of various membership options. Providing members with

specific guidelines, task descriptions, and training can help to gain traction from day one.

- **Tailored volunteering:** Parties should establish centralised coordination of onboarding processes, including tailored offers for initial volunteering. An ideal scenario would be offers that fit into individual activist's time budgets, qualifications, and main fields of interest.

2. Qualify leadership and members

In the coming decades, lifelong training will play a more important role in the labour market. That being said, the focus of professional qualification will shift from the skill level to personal development, such as leadership skills, mediation competence, or awareness practices and stress management. Permanent self-development and training on the personal *and* professional level will be a key factor to professional success.

Organisations who upskill their members develop themselves. Political parties can position themselves as powerhouses of qualification – knowing that individual learning will not only empower each and every party member, but also the organisation as a whole. At the same time, learning in fields like self-leadership, team-leadership or conflict moderation offer an incentive for volunteers to accept party membership.

While not producing tangible benefits in the short term, broad qualification programs will significantly strengthen party structures in the mid and long term. Professional training thus should become the 'new normal' for active members, party officials, and elected representatives. Therefore, parties should introduce their qualification strategies today. They can learn from the business sector, where professional education programs have been implemented for all professional levels over the last decades.

- **Define obligatory competencies for full time officials:** Only those who gained certain professional competencies should be hired.

- **Set targets for qualifying volunteers:** This sets an incentive for the implementation of organisational qualification infrastructures, and helps to promote the organisation's willingness to provide training, coaching and other development measures for their volunteers. Parties should establish a quid pro quo: those who volunteer actively should enjoy qualification benefits, such as training free of cost. And those who enjoy free qualification measures need to be actively engaged in and for the party.
- **Standardising curricula:** Parties need to systematically qualify their elected officials and employees in order to gain increased leadership expertise. One nudge towards that goal would be automatic enrolment for training curricula for all party officials.

3. Diversify

Political parties need diversity on the inside in order to gain legitimacy on the outside. Internal diversity is a precondition to creatively dealing with new social and political developments. It is the most important organisational resource for handling complex challenges. Therefore, diversity is no end in itself for political parties but a strategic imperative.

The ability to talk and listen in a dialogic manner is a prerequisite for mastering diversity, enabling enhanced interaction on the inside, as well as with people and organisations outside of the party.

Along with the readiness for accepting new faces, diversity postulates the readiness to change oneself.[4] The capacity for diversity is synonymous with the capacity for dialogue. Political parties should establish dialogue formats, which deepen the organisational exchange with non-members in order to add to the perspectives on the inside, and to source new ideas and approaches to hitherto unsolved challenges.

- **Strategic dialogues:** This format intensifies the exchange of the party with its environment, expands the scope of policy topics and perspectives, and systematically deepens the network of the party. The format facilitates a change of perspective by bringing together party members with preselected experts, volunteers from other organisations, members of the business community, etc. These dialogues source ideas and impulses on programmatic or organisational questions for the party, and offer networking opportunities and pathways of programmatic influence for non-party participants. Strategic dialogues need a clear thematic focus and a set deadline, as well as explicit expectation management (role definitions, possible impacts, feedback cycles).

- **Inter-sectoral dialogue formats:** Designated party officials on all levels should be responsible for strategically expanding the networks with organisations of other sectors, especially those the party is usually *not* talking with. These people organise regular dialogue formats to foster and deepen exchange.

4. Establish organisational development as permanent duty
Political parties should recognise that promoting and enabling internal innovation is a core task. A smart party promotes innovation labs in order to produce, test, implement and evaluate innovative ideas and initiatives. Designated officials on all levels identify successful party work and help to implement these ideas throughout the organisation.

Innovation needs leadership support in order to bear fruit. The party leadership thus should agree on positive messages regarding attempts to innovate: praise best practices on all levels, promote faces of innovation, and stress the importance of ongoing change for sustaining the party's legitimacy as an agent of change in society.

- **Increase change competence in the party leadership:** Elected officials and full time employees are in charge of developing their organisation (strategy, recruitment, structures and processes, etc). Hence, they should be trained systematically on topics such as leadership, self-management, and organisational development.
- **Use best practices and implement them organisation-wide:** Parties should establish centralised innovation pools where designated officials source, collect and spread innovative projects

and practices. Furthermore, they are responsible for connecting drivers of change and building innovative networks throughout the organisation.

- **Learn from others:** From recruitment to member management and mobilisation, parties should systemically establish learning journeys that take them into realms outside of their own organisational boundaries. One example would be 'exchange programs' for party officials who switch seat with professionals from the NGO or business sector for a week or two.

5. Use technology

Only with a digital infrastructure will parties be able to reconnect and stay connected with civil society. Volunteers need to see a concrete additional value of digital instruments in their daily work in order to successfully implement new digital approaches and tools within the party.

It is important to add that not every technological innovation is useful for political parties – they need to emancipate themselves from the vast number of short lived trends on the digital market in order to spend the limited financial resources wisely.

- **Digital voting:** At party conventions and within individual party bodies, digital votes can help to create a lively feedback culture. These votes are not binding, but an innovative way for elected party leadership to consult their members in real time.
- **Establish prototypes:** Political parties should establish digital prototypes on local and regional level. The prototypes, and the people involved, can serve as a credible reference when rolling out successful projects into bigger parts of the organisation.
- **Digitalisation of member management and communication:** Parties can use digital means to more systematically collect members' and sympathisers' information. This may help to bridge the gap between the party elites and the membership by accelerating the exchange on everyday policy questions. Concerns of data privacy should be addressed by establishing voluntary participation and anonymous storage.

NOTES

1. Claudia Chwalisz, 2015. 'The populist Signal: Why Politics and Democracy need to change'. London: Policy Network, 9; Gerry Stoker, 2013. 'Different Routes to Reforming Politics', in *Political Insight* 4(2), 18–21.

2. The interdisciplinary and trans-party project *Legitimation und Selbstwirksamkeit: Zukunftsimpulse für die Parteiendemokratie* worked 2014/15. Key results in English can be found at www.parteireform.org/die-ergebnisse/.

3. Brian J. Robertson, 2016. *Holacracy: The Revolutionary Management System that abolishes Hierarchy* (London: Portfolio Penguin)

4. See David Bohm, 1999. *On Dialogue*, Oxford: Routledge.

HOW DO WE ENGAGE YOUNG VOTERS?

Georgia Gould

When it comes to young voters we are in an age of post-trust poli-tics. The best way to characterise declining youth turnout is a silent protest. In the thousands of interviews I conducted researching a book on young people and politics, the thread that connected most conversations was anger with the political establishment and a desire for change. Leaders who can give voice to this contempt for the sta-tus quo and offer hope of transformation have the chance of engag-ing young voters. It helps explain why young voters are pointed to as feeding the rise of Jeremy Corbyn, Podemos and Bernie Sanders in one breath and Trump in the other.

But the politics of an emerging generation is not without direction. The European Union referendum of June 2016 helps shine a light on how young people are engaging with politics. Polling suggests that as many as 75 per cent of young people wanted to remain part of the EU. However, it also shows a substantial generation gap in terms of voter turnout between generations.[1]

The substantial remain majority is linked to the fact that Generation Y (born 1980–2000) tend to have a more cosmopolitan outlook than previous generations. Trend data from British Social Attitudes show larger numbers taking a more liberal attitude on a whole range of social issues including immigration. Many are engaging in global online communities around YouTube stars, music, campaigns or a multitude of other niche interests. As the UK's most diverse generation many young people themselves hold complex, multi-layered identities. A group of young men of Somali heritage told me they felt Muslim, Camden, British, Somali and European, with these identities not cancelling each other out but shifting in different circumstances. This diversity can give young people a broader sense of their own identity. Young people were less likely to see immigration as the most important issue in relation to EU membership and far more likely to see the loss of the right to work as a risk of leaving the EU (77 per cent among young voters vs 49 per cent among over 65s according to polling for British Future). This is by no means a universal picture and there are splits on socio-economic status and geography but the tendency is to a more outward looking worldview which translated into support for the EU.

Despite the clear preference among the majority of young voters for remaining in the EU, the referendum failed to engage or inspire this group. In seeking to engage young voters any campaign or party has a huge wall of distrust, cynicism and anger to scale. Most political players and mainstream media outlets have lost their right to be heard with a generation who believe they do not speak to or for them. The EU referendum made little inroads to breaking down this wall. A media narrative largely focused on the wrangling of domestic political players was never going to connect with young voters. The issues they cared about – European travel, work, study and opportunity were buried under a narrative on immigration. There was a lack of young voices debating and sharing their perspective on Europe and a vision that might have inspired them of a modern country with a global outlook. This presented a missed opportunity as a truly youth focused campaign might have encouraged older voters to vote for the sake of their children or grandchildren.

The referendum took place within a wider context in which young voters are neglected and misunderstood. Debate too often focuses on how to deal with their problematic 'apathy' rather than seeking to address the problems with politics that leave them disengaged.

There are underlying issues that help explain this.

The first is the breakdown of entry points into political decision-making for young voters. Not only do many feel ostracised from political institutions, they also feel a lack of belonging and influence in communities and workplaces.

Much analysis says it was ever thus about youth turnout but the figures do not back this up. This generation are less likely than previous generations to vote, identify with a party or engage in civic life. In 1964, 76.4 per cent of those aged under 25 are reported to have voted, the same number as for those aged over 64 years old.[2] In 2015, it was estimated at 43 per cent compared to 78 per cent over 65.[3]

Secondly, the experience of political engagement is very different for young people depending on their background. Research by the Office for National Statistics showed that graduates are three times more likely to engage in civic life.[4] Young people are less likely to identify subjectively with a class but their outcomes in terms of education, participation and opportunity are more likely to be defined by their background. There is a greater premium on education encouraging middle class professionals to invest more and more furiously in their children's education, meaning the state has to do more to equalise opportunities. The problems facing younger generations in terms of access to housing, stable employment and pay progression means that parental support is more important than ever whether it is access to a spare room, guaranteeing a mortgage or support while taking on an unpaid internship. The promise of the internet has been greater equity but for many it has compounded inequalities, with greater opportunities available to those with access to capital and stability. It is no surprise that social mobility is stalling.

Finally, making sense of the individuality that sits beneath so much of young people's political worldview is integral to understanding them. I have lost count of the number of young people who have told me I am not my faith, my class, 'I am just me'. Young people prefer individual acts of expression to formalised involvement whether this is community action, social entrepreneurship or spoken word poetry. They seek to make a direct and personal impact.

This individualism can be a positive force. This is the most entrepreneurial generation we have ever seen with record numbers wanting
to start their own business.[5] Young people who are protective of their
own individuality tend to be more respectful of others. Many express
a desire for a greater purpose and personal impact, and any business
manual on employing millennials will advise a company to demonstrate to younger workers how they are positively benefiting society.

However when combined with lack of opportunity, it can become
a destructive force. When young people are faced with an uncertain
labour market and little opportunity, they do not have a collective
response and are left with blaming others or themselves. A focus
group I did in the Welsh valleys summed this up. These were the
children and grandchildren of trade unionists, all in low paid jobs
or unemployed but wanting more. When I asked them if they ever
thought of joining together politically, one answer summed up the
group response: "What happens if everyone turns up, we're all
together and there is only one job available, everyone's against each
other again." This is a generation that are least likely to be proud of
a welfare state that has not delivered for them and tend to be less
supportive of redistribution than older generations.

This individuality is a huge challenge for leftwing parties who
have found electoral success in appealing to collective identities. In
a recent discussion with a group of young German students they told
me that they felt politically lost as there was no party that represents
the precise interaction of views that make up their personal political
identity. They end up voting for the candidate that seems to offer the
greatest challenge to the status quo. Speaking to them it immediately
resonated with the interviews I conducted with young people across
the UK. There is a fear of a party line, of subsuming their individuality. They are looking for a tailor-made politics which is difficult for
any party (essentially a coalition of views) to offer.

In my view how we find a path towards solidarity in a generation
seeing the world through an individualistic lens is one of the big
questions for the left in modern times. We cannot just continue in
the same vein we were built on that assumed collective identities
and experiences.

HOW DO WE RESPOND?

Addressing instability

We need to respond to the high levels of instability many young people face. Young people live for many years in the private rented sector characterised by unstable tenancies, high prices and lack of protection. As the supply of council housing dwindles, the safety net of secure housing is available to fewer young people. As many young people struggle to meet the basic costs of living, debt becomes a part of life. Research from the Resolution Foundation demonstrates that low pay and lack of career progression is looking to be a chronic and long-term issue for this generation.[6]

At the same time the lack of youth engagement in politics mean young voters and especially disadvantaged young people have bourne much of the brunt of austerity. Analysis by the IPPR revealed that in the 2010 spending review those aged 16 to 24 faced cuts to services worth 28 per cent of their annual household income, compared to just 10 per cent for those aged 55 to 74.[7] It is disadvantaged young people who are least likely to take part and most likely to lose out from policies such as the end of the educational maintenance allowance and housing benefits cuts for under 21s. And young people are left out of new protections such as the increasing minimum wage.

There needs to be a political response that takes up these issues with urgency and power. Many young people are bemused that the services they rely on are silently disappearing. It reinforces their distrust of politics and they need their political leaders to offer some recognition of the challenges they face.

A political agenda that meets the needs of young voters has to include some courage from political leaders about the distribution of resources and some bold national policy agenda such as a comprehensive house building programme. However in addressing these challenges we need to recognise where young people are coming from. This means respecting their desire for individuality and recognising that stability does not necessarily look the same for younger generations as older. Many young people appreciate flexibility in their work so they can pursue a portfolio of careers. A basic income as promoted by Anthony Painter, to use as a platform for entrepreneurial projects will be attractive for some.[8] New models of support and in work training can open up trade unionism to younger people.

Rebuilding our civic space

Responding to the concerns of young voters is not just distributional, it also requires us to act as community builders. Anxiety, stress, loneliness and alienation are rampant issues among the young with 1 in 10 self-harming.[9] It is telling that we have older generations and younger ones struggling with a chronic sense of loneliness.[10] In my local council work I am cabinet member for both young and older people and I hear the same sense of alienation and longing for meaning and belonging across generations. Older people feel scared, many younger people feel judged. They interact through the often poison pen of mainstream media and our communities either disintegrate or never form. People feel trapped in their own homes and public space is eroded. Any political project in the modern age has to be about rebuilding real intergenerational communities. The work of Citizens UK offer an important model based on relational community organising. They allow individuals to be heard and to lead their own campaigns, and at the same time they create intergenerational assemblies to negotiate collective views.

There are increasing numbers of new tech platforms seeking to crowdsource views and promote political dialogue. These platforms have an important role to play in community building but they need investment of time and resource by political leaders. There is no intrinsic rule that means social media is positive for engagement. It can be a space for factional political divisions, anonymous venom and abuse, and most dangerously of all collective delusions where people become imprisoned by the self-reinforcing worldview of their own social networks. As citizens we need to shape our online civic space and create constructive platforms for dialogue. The future of our democracy depends on us all investing time and effort into this.

Political institutions must be part of the solution. This requires nothing less than a bold mission to rebuild our civic space including a programme of institutional reform and the creation of new political institutions that seamlessly integrate on and offline.

Rethinking political engagement

We are not starting from scratch in rethinking political engagement. We can learn from the young people who are already leading this. The most successful youth movements share power and give young people a sense of belonging and ownership. They are not content to be passive recipients of political information, they want to play an active role in decision making. YouTube star and poet Suli Breaks managed to carve out a leadership role for himself not from any position but from leading a global conversation about education through the medium of YouTube videos. He put out an idea, and started an open conversation through YouTube. Young people want to see the same kind of collective endeavour from their policymaking. Participation does not stop with politics and there is an important agenda around championing participation in workplaces through mutual ownership, cooperative principles and employee involvement in governance.

For the hardest to reach young people there has to be real investment in relationship based community organising. This is the hard, community based work of turning up to where young people are, listening, and supporting them to shape their own campaigns. This can be painstakingly slow with those who have least trust and it requires creativity and perseverance. A recent example from a Public Collaboration Lab Camden Council are running with Central Saint Martins (CSM) saw a group of CSM students tasked with redesigning youth centres in some of our most deprived areas. They at first struggled to engage with some of the hard to reach young people who use our services. They tried food, meetings, one to one discussions and were met with silence and resistance. Eventually they took a decision to start dynamically changing the young people's space – moving the pool table, adding new features. The young people responded, writing their feedback, questioning the changes and by the end of the process that silent group had come to present their ideas to the council.

The experience of politics for many can be poor and there is little thought put into how to develop and nurture political activism and invest in young leaders. We lack safe spaces for political dialogue that allow for vulnerability, humanity and nuance. Young people are themselves using the arts as a political tool. A young homeless woman seeking to represent her peers told me that she used poetry, spoken word and art to get their views when words were too difficult. Our work in Camden with CSM shows how art and design can break through traditional political barriers. Students are able to move outside the state-citizen dynamic with all its power dynamics. Design thinking can break outside the for or against nature of much consultation, taking points of tension and turning them into a catalyst for creative solutions.

CONCLUSION

We are far too complacent about our political institutions. It should be a cause of deep concern to anyone in politics that so many of our young people are choosing to believe in conspiracy theories where they are deliberately kept out of power and that the majority of our young citizens are staying away from formal politics. According to Hansard's 2014 audit of political engagement only half of 18 to 24 year olds believe parliamentary institutions are essential for democracy (compared to 73 per cent of those aged over 75).[11] Responding to this requires action at every level. Nationally there should be a new civic jury service where citizens come together across different generations to deliberate together on political issues of local and national concern. Locally community leaders, arts and cultural institutions can provide spaces and forums for dialogue about political and social issues. All of us involved in political and community life have something to contribute, and the starting point is building relationships with young people and reaching out to include them in decision making.

For the progressive left this is an urgent task. Young people grew up in Labour Britain and as a result they are the most tolerant, open and educated generation this country has ever seen. They also face substantial barriers in meeting their high aspirations as a generation. Working with them is both an opportunity for renewal and a chance to embody our values.

NOTES

1. Ipsos mori polling shows a 53 per cent turnout among 18 to 24 year olds compared to 78 of 65 to 74 year olds – Ipsos MORI, 2016. 'The 2016 Referendum Who Was In and Who Was Out' https://www.ipsos-mori.com/researchpublications/researcharchive/3774/The-2016-EU-referendum-who-was-in-and-who-was-out.aspx?view=wide.

2. Aliyah Dar and Adam Mellows-Fraser, 2014. 'Elections: Turnout', Commons Library Standard Note SN01467, p. 4.

3. Ipsos MORI, 2015. 'How Britain Voted in 2015' https://www.ipsos-mori.com/researchpublications/researcharchive/3575/How-Britain-voted-in-2015.aspx.

4. Figen Deviren and Penny Babb, 2005. 'Young People and Social Capital – Phase 2', Office for National Statistics, p. 15 www.google.co.uk/url?q=http://www.ons.gov.uk/ons/guide-method/user-guidance/social-capital-guide/the-social-capital-project/young-people-and-social-capital--phase-2.pdf&sa=U&ved=0ahUKEwiHnpaCtYHMAhXDuhQKHa5rDiU QFggUMAA&sig2=PZ5URVtLB8Ba5_dqtcJbQA&usg=AFQjCNF0hom Zvs5tALaULnFTeF8OExBlTA.

5. Populus / RBS, 2014. 'RBS Enterprise Tracker, In Association with the Centre for Entrepreneurs: 3rd Quarter 2014', p. 27.

6. Adam Corlett and Laura Gardiner, 'Low Pay Britain 2015' (2015) Resolution Foundation Low www.resolutionfoundation.org/wp-content/uploads/2015/10/Low-Pay-Britain-2015.pdf.

7. Sarah Birch, Gelnn Gottfried and Guy Lodge, 2013. 'Divided Democracy – Political Inequality In The UK and Why It Matters' www.ippr.org/files/images/media/files/publication/2013/11/divided-democracy_Nov2013_11420.pdf?noredirect=1.

8. Anthony Painter and Chris Thoung, 2015. 'Creative Citizen, Creative State: The Principled and Pragmatic Case for a Universal Basic Income'. RSA

9. Research in Practice, 2014. 'That Difficult Age: Developing a more effective response to risks in adolescence'. https://www.rip.org.uk/news-and-views/latest-news/evidence-scope-risks-in-adolescence/.

10. ACEVO, 2015. 'Coming In From The Cold - Why We Need to Talk About Loneliness Among Our Young People'. https://www.acevo.org.uk/five-future-creating-prevention-revolution/coming-cold.

11. Hansard Society, 2014. 'Audit of Political Engagement 11: The 2014 Report'. http://doc.ukdataservice.ac.uk/doc/7577/mrdoc/pdf/7577_audit_of_political_engagement_11_2014.pdf.

BEHAVIOURAL INSIGHTS AND THE WELFARE STATE

Tiina Likki

INTRODUCTION

The UK welfare system is characterised by modest welfare benefits, strict entitlement rules and means-tested assistance. This means that most people need to engage with the system in order to gain and maintain access to benefits. In reality, beneficiaries often feel that they have no other option but to engage, which can mean that their contacts with the welfare system are not productive.

To improve engagement, the welfare system needs to understand and incorporate the factors that influence individual judgement, decision making and motivation. We can use new findings from the behavioural sciences to create this engagement, particularly in relation to income support and employment services. For example, in a trial run with Bedford Jobcentre Plus, increasing the personalisation of text messages meant that jobseekers were more likely to attend voluntary job fairs.[1] Similarly, we know that people are influenced by those around them – both for the good and the bad.[2] When people are told that most of those living around them pay their taxes on time, they are more likely to do so themselves.[3] A welfare system that ignores the role of social norms and social influence is likely to perform less well than one that capitalises on social networks and peer support.

Behavioural insights draw on research from across fields as varied as psychology, economics and anthropology to provide a deeper understanding of the drivers of behaviour.[4] Governments around the world increasingly use behavioural science to understand and encourage desirable behaviours such as pension savings, timely tax payments, and healthy eating. Behavioural science is also increasingly applied to different parts of the welfare state, from education and health to income maintenance, often resulting in low-cost and easily scalable interventions. In a study where parents of secondary school pupils were texted regularly about their children's upcoming exams and homework, the children's maths results were boosted by the equivalent of an extra month in the classroom.[5]

Similarly, in welfare policy, we need to understand the factors that influence behaviour and think innovatively about new solutions. For example, in a study done by the Behavioural Insights Team with Loughton Jobcentre Plus, simplifying the Jobcentre process for new claimants and encouraging jobseekers to make specific commitments to future activities increased the percentage of jobseekers no longer claiming benefits by 5 percentage points, and the effect persisted, albeit smaller, when tested across a further 12 Jobcentres.[6]

In addition to using a more realistic and evidence-based model of human behaviour, behavioural insights often draw on rigorous evaluation and innovative approaches to data analysis. For example, an analysis of data on over 120,000 cases relating to social worker decision making in three English local authorities showed, in addition to other findings, that cases were less likely to progress to further action if the referral was received on the weekend.[7] These new analyses can suggest simple changes to improve the way that public services are designed and delivered.

Behavioural insights are also often linked to a commitment to rigorously test the impact of any policy change before deciding whether to implement it at scale. This is based on the view that the public sector has a responsibility both towards the people who will be affected by the policies, and towards tax payers, to ensure they are effective. While not the only option, randomised controlled trials (RCTs) are often used because they provide a high level of confidence that any observed impact was due to the intervention, rather than any other cause.

That said, behavioural insights are not a silver bullet that can always replace existing policy tools such as regulation or providing information. They are best conceived of as fulfilling two functions: first as a complement to traditional policy tools, and second as a lens through which we can evaluate existing or planned policies and improve them.

APPLYING BEHAVIOURAL INSIGHTS AT DIFFERENT LEVELS OF WELFARE POLICY

Behavioural insights can benefit the design and delivery of welfare policy at different levels. At one end, we can use it to inform high level policy design, covering broad questions such as how to structure welfare benefits. At the other end, it can help improve service design, ranging from modifications to the letters people receive and the forms they use to claim benefits, to how they are supported by employment advisors. This is not a hard distinction and there is undoubtedly some overlap in the middle, where policy design translates into service design. The point I wish to make is that, regardless of the level, there is a role for behavioural science as well as rigorous evaluation.

High-level policy design

The first and broadest level relates to high-level policy design. When designing a benefit system, policy makers need to make decisions related to the monetary value of benefits, who is eligible for a certain benefit, and what (if any) conditions apply to receive the benefit. In addition, they must consider if any restrictions should be applied to what the benefit can be used towards (eg voucher or cash based services).

An area that would greatly benefit from an evidence based approach and testing is the impact of conditionality and sanctions on employment outcomes among disabled people and people with health conditions. In a primarily non-disabled population, the evidence on conditionality (eg requiring people to undertake a job search in order to receive benefits) is mixed. It has been shown to have some positive impacts on job entry, but has also been linked to lower earnings and, where sanctions are imposed, to reduced job duration.[8] There is, however, no evidence to suggest that using sanctions to penalise non-compliance (eg failure to attend an interview) leads to better employment outcomes for people with health conditions or disabilities. A trial could test how different degrees of conditionality influence job entry, job duration and earnings. Furthermore, the trial could review any undesirable impacts such as negative effects on wellbeing or mental health.

In an ideal world, these high level policy design choices would be subjected to RCTs or other forms of rigorous evaluation. In practice, however, it is impossible to subject every single element of a policy to a rigorous test, and often policies are rolled out without assessment. Where testing is not possible, either for practical or political reasons, there is still scope for behavioural science to ensure that the principles underpinning the policy are based on an accurate and evidence based understanding of human behaviour. For example, in 2012, decades of concern over low savings rates led to the introduction of automatic enrolment in savings plans in the UK (compared to the past when employees had to actively opt in to take part). To date, the opt-out rates have been very low, with only 9 per cent of workers opting out of a pension scheme and 10 million workers estimated to be newly saving or saving more as a result of automatic enrolment by 2018.[9] This suggests that where in the past psychological inertia led to lower savings it can now be harnessed to ensure fewer people experience poverty later in life.

Service design

The other main way where behavioural insights can be applied is in the design of different government services. As an evidence based approach, behavioural insights can help with two types of questions around service design. The first relates to the practical question of how to get people to engage with the system as it exists. This can involve finding ways to ensure that people take up the services they are entitled to or that they engage fully with the support available. Many people who interact with the government in relation to welfare and employment have an experience that is often bureaucratic and does not take into account individual circumstances. Work done by academics as well as the Behavioural Insights Team, across different policy areas, suggests that some of the key success factors for engagement involve making a behaviour easy, attractive, social and timely.[10] One example from work with Her Majesty's Revenue and Customs showed that directing taxpayers to an online form to be filled out, rather than to a webpage containing the form, could increase response rates significantly.[11] Similar things could be done in welfare provision by making information easy to access, making processes simple to follow, and providing people with the most relevant and personalised information and support.

A factor that makes such changes particularly important relates to psychological scarcity – a phenomenon where the lack of resources such as time or money reduces cognitive bandwidth (ie mental processing capacity) and leads to decisions that may go against an individual's long term interests.[12] This is particularly likely to be the case for people who are struggling to make ends meet or who experience financial or other instability in their lives. From a behavioural perspective, a benefit and employment support system should be designed to reduce the additional burden imposed on already taxed cognitive resources and ensure people can fully engage with the support available.

The second question that behavioural insights can help address in relation to service design is to assess and ensure that the support offered leads to the desired employment outcomes. Even when a new intervention or service is designed based on evidence, it should be tested to ensure it has the desired impact in the target population. An example of an innovative RCT to improve the effectiveness of job searches by using a low cost online tool comes from a team of economists led by Michele Belot. In a study of jobseekers in Scotland, the researchers asked half the participants to use an alternative job search platform that offered tailored suggestions to broaden the person's job search to occupations they might not have considered on their own. The study found that the jobseekers who used the new interface experienced a 30 per cent increase in job interviews.[13]

Recommendations for policymakers

The findings presented above offer insights into the behavioural dynamics of welfare policy and service delivery but much more can be done. A behaviourally informed approach points to three concrete steps that policymakers can take:

1. Understand the user experience
2. Apply behavioural science
3. Evaluate and iterate

The first step is to become genuinely familiar with how engaging with a service feels from a user's perspective. Liaising with charities and user groups can prove invaluable for making visible the frictions and inconsistencies that may seem small from the policymaker's perspective but deeply impact how people engage with a service. Embarking on the customer journey oneself, whether trying to make a claim or set up an account without having access to a computer, can also be revealing.

This step is relevant, for example, to Universal Credit, the new welfare system in the UK, which introduces greater work coach discretion to decide the level of conditionality applied to an individual who receives benefits. The first step to ensure this element of the system is designed appropriately entails observing what information work coaches draw on to make these decisions, whether different work coaches provided with the same information make the same decision, and whether different customers have the same ability to describe their capability to work and to advocate for themselves.

The second step is to explore the behavioural literature to understand what findings from behavioural science could explain why a policy or a service works well, and why it does not. In employment and welfare policy, this often means looking beyond research that is most directly linked to these areas and making creative connections with behavioural studies in other fields, such as health or education. In the case of decision-making among Universal Credit work coaches, this could entail looking at the evidence from behavioural science regarding confirmation bias (where people focus on information that is in line with their existing beliefs) or risk aversion (the tendency to avoid risk under uncertainty).

Finally, any new service change or intervention would ideally be evaluated at a smaller scale before any wider implementation. To create a well-functioning and personalised system of support for people who receive benefits, the system should ensure that discretion in setting conditionality does not have unintended consequences. This could mean providing work coaches with tools to support decision-making and then testing whether using them results in better wellbeing and employment outcomes for the people they are meant to help.

NOTES

1. Michael Sanders and Elspeth Kirkman, 2014. "I've booked you a place. Good luck: a field experiment applying behavioural science to improve attendance at high-impact recruitment events." Centre for Market and Public Organisation, working paper no. 13/334, http://www.bristol. ac.uk/medialibrary/sites/cmpo/documents/WebVersion.pdf.

2. Robert B. Cialdini and Melanie R. Trost, 1998. "Social influence: Social norms, conformity and compliance," in *The Handbook of Social Psychology*, ed. Daniel T. Gilbert, Susan T. Fiske, and Lindzey Gardner (New York: McGraw-Hill), 151.

3. Michael, Hallsworth, John, List, Robert Metcalfe and Ivo Vlaev, 2014. "The behavioralist as tax collector: Using natural field experiments to enhance tax compliance," *National Bureau of Economic Research*, no. w20007.

4. I use the term 'behavioural insights' to refer to the approach used by the Behavioural Insights Team and other similar organisations that draws on a range of behavioural sciences to improve policy design, as well as often places a lot of importance on evaluation. I use the term 'behavioural science' to refer to the body of research that behavioural insights draws on.

5. Sarah Miller et al., 2016. "Texting parents. Evaluation report and executive summary." (Evaluation report, Education Endowment Foundation).

6. "The Behavioural Insights Team Update Report 2013–15", accessed November 6, 2016, http://www.behaviouralinsights.co.uk/publications/the-behavioural-insights-team-update-report-2013-2015/.

7. Alex Tupper et al., 2016. "Decision-making in children's social care. Quantitative data analysis." (Report, Department for Education).

8. Patrick Arni, Rafael Lalive, and Jan C. Van Ours, 2013. "How effective are unemployment benefit sanctions? Looking beyond unemployment exit." *Journal of Applied Econometrics* 28, no. 7: 1153–1178.

9. Department for Work and Pensions, 2016. "Employers' Pension Provision survey 2015" (Department for Work and Pensions research report No 919); Department for Work and Pensions, 2016. "Workplace pensions: Update on analysis on Automatic Enrolment 2016" (Department for Work and Pensions)

10. Owain Service et al., 2014. "EAST: Four simple ways to apply behavioural insights," Behavioural Insights Team, http://www.behaviouralinsights.co.uk/publications/east-four-simple-ways-to-apply-behavioural-insights/.

11. Service et al, "EAST."

12. Sendhil Mullainathan and Eldar Shafir, 2013. *Scarcity: Why Having Too Little Means So Much* (New York: Times Books).

13. Michèle Belot, Philipp Kircher, and Paul Muller, 2015. "Providing Advice to Job Seekers at Low Cost: An Experimental Study on On-Line Advice," *CEPR Discussion Papers* 10967, www.cepr.org/active/publications/discussion_papers/dp.php?dpno=10967.

LOCATION, LOCATION, LOCATION

Building place-based system change for better social outcomes

Anna Randle

Public services have traditionally been designed to solve society's problems. A health service to treat illness. Police to step in when people are not safe. Drug and alcohol services to cure people of their addictions. Social services to look after people who, for various reasons, cannot look after themselves. And on it goes: a complex arrangement of publicly funded services. Some are delivered to everyone, some only to those who need them; some are controlled locally, some nationally – with accountability varying just as much.

Public services play a critical role in helping and protecting citizens. But we know something is not working. Demand for public services is ever-increasing, driven in part by an ageing population and changing public expectations. At a time when costs are rising, the funding for local public services is being massively reduced by central government. Fundamentally, public services are not solving our most intractable social and economic challenges. Inequalities in health and education outcomes and economic participation are rising. There is huge variation in the economic and social outcomes of different towns and cities in the UK, and even within neighbourhoods. Communities in which the most public money is spent continue to place the highest demand on services over time. And we know that individuals and families with the most complex needs experience multiple interventions from different services and agencies, and yet all too often remain trapped in repeating cycles of intervention, and often in intergenerational patterns of need and deprivation.

Public services need to change. But how?

Collaborate's work with local authorities and other local public services across the country has generated two key insights:

1. The causes of social problems are complex and interrelated.
2. There is often a geographic, or place based, dimension.

These insights lead us to two conclusions that have deep implications for our understanding of the role of local public services:

First, that addressing complex problems requires the contribution of many different actors, and no single service, organisation or person can address the root causes of need alone.

Consider the health outcomes for adult men in a particular ward of a city. Data tell us that the health outcomes for men in this ward are worse than in a different part of the city. The reasons for this disparity are complex. They are likely to include, for example, levels of employment, access to education and training, diet, access to green space, exercise and lifestyle, income and the social norms and expectations men experience in their community.

Addressing those root causes requires the contribution of many different actors and organisations. From the perspective of public services, this might be about utilising the collective resource of housing, work training and employment services, welfare, local GPs and so on. These services have the potential to be more impactful if they are pulling in the same direction, working in similar ways and collaborating to provide more holistic support to people in the community.

Second, that many parts of the solution also exist at a local level – be it the individual, the family, the community, the neighbourhood, the town or the city – so local public service organisations should build place-based approaches that take into account the reality of people's lives where they live.

We know that people's own motivation and drive to change is critical and that significant spheres of influence on outcomes exist within families, networks and communities. For example, families and friends influence people's behaviour and choices, and communities establish subtle social norms, or provide sources of social support. These are spheres of influence that public services traditionally do not to think about, or have tackled principally through national campaigns.

However, to return to the example above, we must acknowledge that not even the council or local NHS partners, with their relatively large budgets and workforce, can solve complex social challenges such as inequalities in health outcomes simply through delivering services.

It is therefore critical that public services look for potential resources in the wider community, in institutions such as churches, voluntary sector groups, local businesses, social networks and even families. This is not about the 'heavy hand of the state' reaching into our living rooms, but about understanding where community assets can be recognised, valued and included as part of the system that can positively influence an outcome.

Through our research, we have identified a number of things that we believe should be explicitly recognised and deployed by public service organisations as part of the route to improved social and economic outcomes in our communities:

- **Community engagement and relationship building**: enabling people working in public services to understand what is happening in people's lives and within communities - the root causes of demand, not simply the presenting problems
- **Identifying and working with local community assets**: people (like community leaders and people of influence, such as faith leaders) and places (buildings and outside spaces where people can convene and do things together, such as growing food, cooking, and sport)
- **Identifying other organisations with a role to play**: for example, voluntary groups and third sector organisations that can bring people together; businesses that can be encouraged to act in more socially responsible ways

- **Mobilising citizens and building social networks**: so that people feel part of a community, can help each other, find informal support from their neighbours and connect with people with similar interests - what Julia Unwin describes as the "frontline defence against poverty"
- **Building community capacity and resilience**: for example, through asset-based community development
- **Influencing behaviours and social norms**: for example, working with local parents to encourage them to socialise, play and read with their children
- **Redesigning frontline public services so that they act as part of this local ecosystem**: for example, GP surgeries socially prescribing community activities and hosting local groups; children's centres that help parents grow local networks; social workers and housing officers who can take the time to understand the root causes of people's needs, the strengths and assets they have and the role of community connections as part of the solution; and integrated frontline teams of different public services and community development capacity.

BEHAVING LIKE A SYSTEM: SHIFTING OUR UNDERSTANDING OF PUBLIC SERVICES

Based on these conclusions, we think there are four shifts that we need to make in the way that we think about how we change outcomes in communities and the role of public services:

- Change the assumption that public services alone can solve people's problems
- Reconceive public services as part of a place-based system that can influence outcomes, including people, families, communities, local organisations and institutions, the third sector and businesses
- Consider how the collective power of that system can be mobilised to address a common cause

• Use public money to invest in, build, and influence that system to support and enable other parts of the system to play a role in achieving positive change

These shifts help us to understand the case for collaboration between different public services, as well as the importance of building productive relationships among the statutory sector and other bodies (such as community and voluntary organisations), and with communities themselves.

The benefits of whole system, whole place collaboration

Working as a place-based system presents the opportunity to build new, collaborative routes to better social outcomes. As part of this, we think that it also creates opportunities to rethink other assumptions that underpin the way we have approached place-based change in the past.

From services to outcomes in a place

First, we can think holistically about how outcomes in a place are achieved, beyond service and organisational silos. Joined-up services mean the accountability of individual public service institutions then shifts from the quality of the services they deliver to the quality of outcomes in a place. For example, can it be right that a hospital can achieve a top rating for the quality of its services if it is in an area with poor health outcomes? What would a genuinely systemic approach to place based health look like?

Towards integrated public service reform and economic growth

Second, we should build more integrated approaches to public service reform and economic development. Many of the determinants of people's ability to access and benefit from economic growth are social and cultural, and yet we tend to focus on the physical (such as transport infrastructure), the service based (such as JobCentre Plus) or even the punitive (such as welfare reform). How could we use public service resources to build people's confidence and capacity to access jobs, creating the preconditions for inclusive growth?

From efficiency gains for one organisation to demand management across a system

Thirdly, a whole system approach enables public service organisations to shift from focusing on efficiency gains (or cuts) for individual organisations to thinking about demand management across a whole system of services. How can we align the financial incentives of different parts of the public sector better? And what is the cross sector investment case for integrated, place-based investment in community networks and activity as one means of managing demand for services?

From political vision for the council to political vision for the place

Finally, we can move from a political vision for the council towards a political vision for place. A shared strategic plan for all local public services will underpin this vision, while investment and democratic accountability for a wider range of local services will be crucial in order to realise it.

WHAT DOES THIS MEAN LOCAL PUBLIC SERVICES NEED TO DO?

This is easy to say and hard to do, particularly at scale. Such place-based collaboration too often remains an ambition, getting stuck at the margins in interesting but small scale pilots and projects, of which there are many examples. We need the organisations that have the most influence over how public services are run and the financial resources to build and sustain local systems to take the time to understand and purposefully build the system infrastructure that will translate aspirational words into new practice.

Key aspects of the local authority role in place-based system change include:

- convening partners throughout the system
- designing a process through which new principles and behaviours for public services are defined
- leading politically and co-creating a social and economic vision for the future of the place
- mobilising citizens and supporting/helping to create social movements (or acting as a local 'platform' for change)
- testing new ways of working, with a view to creating deeper and broader change based on insights and learning
- building the 'system infrastructure', or hard wiring, that will enable the translation of ambition into new collaborative culture and practice

From Collaborate's research with public services and a range of other stakeholders in several places, we have identified nine building blocks of 'place-based system infrastructure'. We have designed a framework for local authorities and other local public services to help them to understand what they need to change in order to shift from silo organisations to a genuinely collaborative, place-based approach.

The nine building blocks themselves, including place-based strategy, funding, governance, accountability, data, delivery and workforce strategy, are not revelatory - they are the things we would all recognise as determining how organisations work and the experience of using local public services. However, when considered through the lens of place based collaboration, their function is significantly different. Redesigning and repurposing existing institutional infrastructure to support place based collaboration is a critical part of building new local public services that can tackle complex social problems and, most importantly, better social and economic outcomes in our communities.

CONCLUSION

In our experience, the question of how different institutions and people in places can collaborate for better social outcomes already underpins much of the work going on to improve public services and outcomes up and down the country. A number of places have already begun the work of creating a new account of the role of place-based public services and institutions: less paternal, more empowering; prioritising local collaboration over centralised hierarchies; holistic not fragmented, and facilitating the contribution of citizens and a broad range of organisations and activities to improve outcomes. But at the moment, these tend to be peripheral to public service systems that are continuing largely as before. In our experience only a very small number of places (Oldham in Greater Manchester is a good example), are attempting change across the whole system and whole place.

This is beginning to change, due to austerity, rising demand, post-Brexit self-reflection about communities that have been 'left behind', and the potential opportunities afforded by devolution. We at Collaborate think that the work of the next period will be to support this change by helping local public services to shift how they think, behave and work. We will help them to build new relationships and, fundamentally, a new practice and culture based on a different understanding of how we can create new routes to social change in our communities.

Collaborate CIC is a cutting edge social business that helps services, systems and communities collaborate to improve social and economic outcomes. www.collaboratei.com

SOCIAL MOBILITY AND NONCOGNITIVE SKILLS

Charlie Cadywould

Previous progressive governments have attempted to tackle inequality of opportunity primarily through redistribution of income and investment in public services. The belief has been that if we ensure children don't grow up in poverty, have a high quality comprehensive education system and widen access to higher education, the entrenched class system can gradually be eroded. In this chapter, I argue that without a proper understanding of how class advantages are transferred between generations, particularly the transmission of noncognitive skills, we will never achieve equality of opportunity.

Recent political interest in noncognitive skills, or 'character', has inspired a wave of studies and pilot programmes that demonstrate how these skills reinforce inequality at each stage of life: they affect cognitive development, educational attainment, and labour market outcomes. Moreover, there is mounting evidence that these non-cognitive skills can be developed through interventions both in and outside of the classroom. However, it appears that political support for the character agenda has peaked, attention in education policy circles is shifting, and it is in danger of becoming just another 'fad'. The final section of this chapter tackles some of the recent criticisms that have emerged of the character agenda as it has developed in the US as well as the UK. Ultimately, I argue, unequal development of noncognitive skills is an early symptom of class disadvantage, and must be tackled alongside efforts to reduce the more entrenched causes: social and economic inequality.

SOCIAL MOBILITY

The statistics on social mobility in the UK are stark. The odds of an individual being in the highest social class group by the age of thirty are around 20 times higher for an individual born into that same social class than for someone born into the lowest class.[1] People at the 90th percentile of family background income have expected earnings around 53 per cent higher than those at the 10th percentile.[2] Numerous comparative studies have found the UK to be less mobile than other advanced economies.[3]

There is a commonly deployed narrative of a 'golden age of social mobility' after 1945 followed by a decline towards the end of the 20th century. The academic literature backs up the 'golden age' hypothesis in absolute terms, though the 'decline' is perhaps exaggerated. The rapid expansion of professional and managerial positions created more room at the top, giving those from low income or class backgrounds a greater chance of moving into a better paid, middle class occupation than previous generations. This expansion slowed down in the 1980s and 1990s, and the popular perception of a squeeze was probably exacerbated by men facing greater competition from women for those positions.[4]

However, the evidence for changing relative social mobility – that is, the likelihood of an individual substantially changing their social position from birth to adulthood relative to the rest of the population – is more contested. Paterson and Iannelli's analysis of the British Household Panel Survey found that social mobility did not change substantially between pre-war, baby-boomer and subsequent generations.[5] On the other hand, Blanden's work on the British Cohort Studies found that the adult earnings of those born in 1970 were more strongly associated with their family incomes than the earnings of those born in 1958. [6] Similarly, MacMillan finds an increasing trend for those born into richer families becoming lawyers and doctors between the two cohorts.[7] This suggests a decline in relative income mobility between the two time points. More recent, short term data published by the Social Mobility Commission suggest social mobility is flatlining or declining according to various indicators.[8]

NONCOGNITIVE SKILLS

The causes of persisting social immobility are complex. Blanden, Gregg and Macmillan's 2007 analysis of the British Cohort Studies focused on the transmission of advantage in the labour market between parents and children, focusing on cognitive skills (literacy and numeracy), 'noncognitive skills' (including self-esteem, application and 'locus of control') and educational outcomes. All of these were found to be associated with socioeconomic background. The study concluded that the power of cognitive and noncognitive skills in childhood to predict adult earnings are roughly equal, and that the impact of noncognitive skills in particular appears to be mediated through educational attainment.[9] They also found that these skills are particularly important for disadvantaged young people: a child from a deprived background with strong 'application' at age 10 typically has 14 per cent higher earnings at age 30 than other deprived children. The figure among children from more affluent backgrounds is just 4 per cent.[10]

Blanden's UK studies in the mid-2000s, along with those of Heckman, Duckworth and others in the US opened up academic interest in the role of what have variously been called noncognitive skills, social and emotional skills, and character. These are a set of personality traits, virtues or skills that have been shown to affect a wide range of later life outcomes including educational attainment, income, occupation, mental health, life satisfaction, wellbeing, physical health, obesity, smoking, crime, marriage and mortality.[11]

The list of traits and skills associated with these outcomes is even longer, including among many others: self-control, grit, creativity, resilience, empathy, application, communication, self-awareness, organisation, confidence, conscientiousness, self-efficacy, motivation and critical thinking.[12]

These might sound like buzzwords, but the evidence that something real and important lies behind them is robust. In relation to labour market outcomes, the impact of noncognitive skills operates at least on three levels. First, cognitive and noncognitive skills have been shown to be interdependent; developing one promotes development in the other. In turn, cognitive skills are associated with educational and labour market outcomes. [13]

Second, noncognitive skills are proven to promote educational outcomes, even after controlling for cognitive skills. A recent study conducted in the US found that traits such as openness to experience, conscientiousness and agreeableness are more predictive of school grades than IQ. [14] Angela Duckworth's work on the concept of 'grit' also finds a strong correlation with grades.[15]

Finally, in line with Blanden's original findings, noncognitive skills have a direct impact on labour market outcomes, beyond the mediated impact they have through cognitive skills and educational attainment. In other words, a child with superior noncognitive skills typically has higher earnings and is more likely to work in the higher professions than their peers with inferior noncognitive skills, but similar exam results and levels of numeracy and literacy. For example, Claire Tyler's 2016 study assesses the relative contribution of four potential transmission mechanisms for the children of parents employed in the higher professions: cognitive skills, noncognitive skills, job aspirations and educational attainment. Overall, the children of parents employed in a top job are 22.8 percentage points more likely to access a top job in adulthood than the children of other parents.[16] She finds that childhood cognitive skills (literacy and numeracy at age 10) account for 20 per cent of the intergenerational persistence in top-job status, while a range of noncognitive skills account for 9 per cent. When educational outcomes are added to the model, noncognitive skills still account for 5 per cent of the family background disparity.[17]

CAN WE CHANGE OUR CHARACTER?

An understanding of the influence of personality traits on outcomes reveals the limits of conventional approaches to promoting social mobility. For example, a drive to ensure educational achievement at the age of 16 is no longer influenced by social background would be both doomed and insufficient to ensure even labour market outcomes unless social background differences in noncognitive skills could also be addressed. The same could be said for a drive to address the relationship between social background and numeracy and literacy. Indeed, if it turned out that character traits are more or less fixed at birth, then full social mobility, and equality of opportunity, would be a utopian dream.

Some noncognitive skills do appear to be largely inherited. The Education Endowment Foundation's literature review argues that certain, more deeply ingrained, personality traits like grit and creativity are hard to alter.[18] However, more context specific traits such as motivation and engagement, as well as skills like self-control are fairly malleable.[19] Numerous studies have shown that that character is, in fact, heavily dependent on upbringing and schooling, and can be developed with interventions both in and outside of the classroom.

First, there is evidence that private schools develop character. While caveating their conclusions with the fact that it is impossible to control for possible character bias in private school selection processes, Green et al. find that private school pupils have more 'locus of control' than state school pupils, controlling for social background and prior cognitive skills.[20] In a later study, Green found that, again accounting for social background, privately educated workers are more likely to be in jobs requiring significantly greater leadership skills, offer greater organisational participation and require greater work intensity.[21]

Second, findings from the Great Smoky Mountains Study of Youth in North Carolina reveal the effect of cash injections on character; the study is both remarkable and impossible to replicate. Initially tracking the personalities of 1,420 low income children, by good fortune, a quarter of the children's families were given an additional $4,000 a year as members of a Native American community owed compensation during the lifetime of the study – this effectively gave researchers a real-life, large-sample randomised control trial. Those who received the extra cash boosted conscientiousness and agreeableness, both of which are correlated with later life success and happiness.[22]

Finally, as the evidence on the importance of character has developed, so has the evidence base around interventions designed to develop it. The Education Endowment Foundation cites studies showing that mentoring, service learning, outdoor adventure, and dedicated social and emotional learning programmes can improve noncognitive skills on a number of measures.[23] Recent evaluations of pilot programmes funded by the Department for Education have also seen positive results.[24]

THE CHARACTER AGENDA

Just at the point where the evidence base has matured, and attention has turned from the effects of strong noncognitive skills to the causes and interventions that might build them, there are signs that the character agenda is beginning to wane. At its peak, perhaps, with David Cameron's Life Chances Strategy, it does not appear to be a priority for Theresa May's domestic agenda. Two of its strongest political proponents in the UK – Nicky Morgan and Tristram Hunt, at one point Education Secretary and Shadow Education Secretary respectively – have withdrawn from positions of political leadership. Grants to pilot and expand programmes to improve character were worth £3m in 2015, and expanded to £6m in 2016, but in June 2016 it was announced that a third of this pot would be dedicated to military-style projects, which has strong support among conservative commentators, but for which the evidence is severely limited: the government's own review "identified a range of issues which, together undermine the potential for impacts to be attributed to the Military Ethos programme in a form which would stand up to external scrutiny."[25] Furthermore, as of March 2017, the 2016 character grants are yet to be distributed, amid fears that they could be scrapped.

Aside from a general sense that the government has pivoted to focusing on and prioritising Brexit negotiations since Theresa May's elevation to the premiership, the education debate has moved on too. The reintroduction of grammar schools opens up old political divisions previously thought long healed as a result of overwhelming evidence against them. With the Labour leadership opposing both grammars and the academy system, we are back to a debate about institutions, while content takes a back seat.

There is therefore a risk that the character agenda will run out of steam and be remembered as just another fad. Indeed, a number of criticisms of the character agenda have recently emerged, which could begin to take hold.

OBJECTIONS

The blame game

The first is that instead of trying to tackle structural inequalities such as in educational provision or discriminatory or exclusive recruitment processes, the character agenda essentially blames poor people for being poor. This is especially problematic with character traits like self-control. Consider the infamous marshmallow test: children are told they can eat a marshmallow in front of them, or wait a while and get two. If they can wait, it is said, they are displaying the ability to 'delay gratification', which is associated with good grades and higher earnings.[26] Subsequent versions of the test have shown that the ability to wait is heavily dependent on prior life experience, and that the decision not to wait can be a rational decision. In one experiment, a group of children experienced a promise being kept (provision of new crayons) by the researcher, while for another group the promise was broken. Children who had had a promise kept were able to wait significantly longer for the second marshmallow than those who had had the promise broken.[27] Children who grow up in unstable, unpredictable environments might be making a similarly 'rational' choice in not delaying gratification. Moreover, there might be times in later life where the situation is uncertain and it is also 'rational' to take what you can get as soon as you can get it.

This is a legitimate criticism of the marshmallow test: the researcher has access to information (the second marshmallow really is forthcoming) that the child does not. It is also a possible criticism of the desirability of a trait like delaying gratification. Not delaying gratification might have benefits in certain situations, to which any interventions designed to improve the ability to delay gratification would have to be sensitive.

However, it doesn't mean that teaching character is not a worthy endeavour. It reminds us that we have to be careful about exactly what kinds of traits we are teaching, and how. In fact, though, it underlines a key point: that noncognitive skills are to an extent determined by social background[28] makes it all the more clearly unjust that they are unevenly distributed. It is not that some people just innately have 'good character' and some don't, it is that people's backgrounds can affect noncognitive skills just like cognitive skills. Both affect life prospects, so why should they be treated any differently?

It also reveals that developing noncognitive skills can't be a replacement for tackling issues like child poverty. This revised marshmallow test, like the Smoky Mountains study, shows that noncognitive skills can be better developed under certain social and economic conditions. Moreover, none of the literature claims that disparities in noncognitive skills explain social immobility in its totality. There is a great body of literature, including the 'Great Gatsby Curve' showing a clear link between higher levels of economic inequality and social immobility in a society.[29] Tackling the character gap doesn't mean we have to abandon goals like eradicating child poverty or reducing inequality.

Crowding out numeracy and literacy

The second criticism is that it crowds out other important facets of education. Teachers are under ever more pressure to deliver good exam results for their pupils. When the evidence on the interventions that work is still developing, it's understandable that teachers might see it as a luxury they can't afford. Many schools and teachers feel they already teach character through a school ethos and interactions with pupils. Some feel it adds to the burden on pupils if they are being directly taught about noncognitive skills. Education writer Valerie Strauss argues of the debate around 'grit' in the US:

> "The grit discourse is driven primarily not be concerns about disadvantaged students but by the anxiety of middle and upper-class parents about the character of their own children. The critics, however, are right that poor children are the inevitable losers of this game. An overemphasis on character education means that fewer resources will be spent on teaching disadvantaged students the skills and knowledge they need to actually succeed academically and professionally. Sisyphus had plenty of grit, but it didn't get him very far."[30]

This ignores two of the key insights from the academic evidence: first, that noncognitive skills have a positive effect on cognitive skills and educational outcomes, and second, that noncognitive skills have been shown to be substantially more important for disadvantaged children than their more affluent peers. On the other hand, it does raise an important question of the measure the relative success of various programmes or teaching styles. For example, developing noncognitive skills might help to develop cognitive skills such as numeracy, but is an extra hour of character development more effective at improving numeracy than an extra hour of maths? Probably not, so we need to consider the full range of outcomes when we decide what to prioritise in education.

Morality and the state

The final objection relates to morality. The character agenda has been criticised as both too moralistic and not moralistic enough. On the one hand, Jeffrey Aaron Snyder argues that character education:

> "promotes an amoral and careerist 'looking out for number one' point of view . . . today's grit and self-control are basically industry and temperance in the guise of psychological constructs rather than moral imperatives. Why is this distinction important? While it takes grit and self-control to be a successful heart surgeon, the same could be said about a suicide bomber."[31]

This may be a fair criticism of some character programmes in the US, but in the UK character has developed a distinctly moral flavour, in part thanks to the influential Jubilee Centre for Character and Virtues.[32]

Others object to character, particularly the term itself, because it has the air of something old-fashioned, elitist, and conservative or even militaristic.[33] It evokes out-of-date ideas about 'character building' punishments, the 'stiff upper lip' and 'tough love'.

This is primarily a problem of politics and branding. Character might have been the best term to bring conservatives to a cause which might otherwise have been seen as a bit paternalistic, obsessively egalitarian, 'alternative', or just a bit soft or wishy-washy. But in calling it character, it might have put off some teachers who see it as a further ideological interference by a Conservative government which has previously displayed hostility towards the profession. On the other hand, this branding may have had a real influence on how the agenda has been shaped: it might explain why funding for character has been pushed into 'military ethos' provision, despite the lack of evidence for its effectiveness.

Others reject the idea that there is a single set of personality traits that should be desirable, or at least that it is the role of the state to decide what is and isn't. As one teacher puts it:

> "By trying to make Character . . . a thing that can be taught explicitly, measured, reported on, with data collected and dispersed to all and sundry, it could be said that the very idea of 'character' is transmuted from being a collection of difficult to define human traits that might emerge over time, to that of a bureaucrat's idea of character."[34]

There is certainly a grain of truth in this as it relates to Goodhart's Law: when a measure becomes a target, it is no longer a useful measure. There is a challenge to ensure that the character agenda does not become another inefficient box-ticking exercise. However, the wider point about whether 'bureaucrats' should involve themselves at all depends entirely on the kinds of character traits the state is trying to instil. This raises difficult and complex questions – it must avoid totalitarian-style indoctrination, for example – but if done right, character education can help guard future generations against indoctrination from other sources. Teaching children to be questioning, curious, motivated and equipped to pursue the truth, can do exactly that.

CONCLUSION

Governments that want to tackle social immobility should follow the evidence. Research shows that the gap in noncognitive skills among children from deprived and more affluent backgrounds play an important role in Britain's lack of intergenerational social mobility. More recent research shows that noncognitive skills – or character – can be developed through interventions from early years to young adulthood, both in and outside of formal educational settings. However, despite the promise of the character agenda, which until recently had gained significant and active support from both main political parties, it is in danger of becoming just another passing fad.

While there are legitimate questions and concerns about the way character is taught, and the kinds of traits and skills that should be taught, otherwise instilled, and ultimately measured, the evidence should not be ignored. It is not good enough for children from deprived families to be consigned to inferior life chances while those attending private schools gain an additional edge in the labour market beyond better grades. We must not forget the role that growing up in poverty plays in disadvantaging children at every stage, but there is more than one route to tackling this disadvantage. We need an 'all of the above' approach to achieving social mobility: tackle the causes of disadvantage, but tackle the early symptoms too.

NOTES

1. Patrick Sturgis, 2015. *Trends in Social Mobility in the UK – Evidence Briefing*, University of Southampton, p. 2. Available at: http://www.sut-tontrust.com/wp-content/uploads/2015/12/Evidence-Briefing-Trends-in-Social-Mobility-in-the-UK-Professor-Patrick-Sturgis.pdf.

2. Silvia Mendolia and Peter Siminski, 2016. 'Does Family Background Affect Earnings through Education? A Generalised Approach to Mediation Analysis', *IZA Discussion Paper Series*, no. 9917.

3. Jo Blanden, 2013. 'Cross-national rankings of intergenerational mobility: a comparison of approaches from economics and sociology', *Journal of Economic Surveys*, 27(1), pp. 38–73.; OECD, 2010. 'A Family Affair: Intergenerational Social Mobility across OECD Countries', in *Economic Policy Reforms: Going for Growth*, OECD, pp. 183–200.

4. John Goldthorpe, 2012. 'Understanding – and Misunderstanding – Social Mobility in Britain: The Entry of the Economists, the Confusion of Politicians and the Limits of Educational Policy', *Barnett Papers in Social Research*, available at: https://www.spi.ox.ac.uk/fileadmin/docu-ments/PDF/Goldthorpe_Social_Mob_paper_01.pdf.

5. Goldthorpe, 'Understanding – and Misunderstanding – Social Mobility in Britain'; Lindsay Paterson and Cristina Iannelli, 2007. 'Patterns of Absolute and Relative Social Mobility: A Comparative Study of England, Wales and Scotland.' *Sociological Research Online*, no. 12(6)15, pp. 1–21.

6. Jo Blanden, Paul Gregg and Stephen Machin, 2005. 'Intergenerational Mobility in Europe and North America', *Centre for Economic Performance*. Available at: http://www.suttontrust.com/wp-content/uploads/2005/04/IntergenerationalMobility.pdf; Jo Blanden, Paul Gregg and Lindsey Macmillan, 2007. 'Accounting for Intergenerational Income Persistence: Noncognitive Skills, Ability and Education', *The Economic Journal,* no. 117, pp. 43–60.

7. Lindsey MacMillan, 2009. *Social Mobility and the Professions*, submission to the Panel for Fair Access to the Professions, Centre for Market and Public Organisation. Available at http://www.bristol.ac.uk/media-library/sites/cmpo/migrated/documents/socialmobility.pdf.

8. Social Mobility Commission, 2016. *State of the Nation 2016: Social Mobility in Great Britain*, Social Mobility Commission.

9. Blanden et al. 'Accounting for Intergenerational Income Persistence: Noncognitive Skills, Ability and Education'.

10. Jonathan Birdwell, Ralph Scott and Louis Reynolds, 2015. *Character Nation,* Demos. Available at: https://www.demos.co.uk/project/character-nation-2/. Derived from Blanden et al. 'Accounting for Intergenerational Income Persistence: Noncognitive Skills, Ability and Education'.

11. Alissa Goodman, Heather Joshi, Bilal Nasim and Claire Tyler, 2015. *Social and Emotional Skills in Childhood and their Long-Term Effects on Adult Life: A Review for the Early Intervention Foundation,* Institute of Education .

12. Birdwell et al., *Character Nation*; Emma Garcia, 2014. 'The Need to Address Noncognitive Skills in the Education Policy Agenda', *Economic Policy Institute Briefing Papers,* no. 386.

13. Garcia, 'The Need to Address Noncognitive Skills in the Education Policy Agenda'; Emma Garcia, 2013. 'What we learn in school: Cognitive and non-cognitive skills in the educational production function' [PhD thesis, Columbia University]. Available at: https://www.researchgate.net/publication/259183954_What_we_learn_in_school_Cognitive_and_non-cognitive_skills_in_the_educational_production_function.

14. Lex Borghans, Bart Golsteyn, James Heckman and John Humphries, 2016. 'What Grades and Achievement Tests Measure', *Proceedings of the National Academy of Sciences of the United States of America*, vol. 113(47), pp. 13354–13359. Available at: http://www.pnas.org/content/113/47/13354.full.pdf.

15. Angela Duckworth, Christopher Peterson, Michael Matthews and Dennis Kelly, 2007. 'Grit: Perseverance and Passion for Long-Term Goals', Journal of Personality and Social Psychology, vol.92(6), pp. 1087–1101.

16. Claire Tyler, 2016. 'The role of non-cognitive and cognitive skills in accounting for the intergenerational transmission of "top job" status', *Department of Quantitative Social Science Working Papers*, no. 16(3).

17. Tyler, 'The role of non-cognitive and cognitive skills in accounting for the intergenerational transmission of "top job" status'.

18. Leslie Morrison Gutman and Ingrid Schoon, 2013. *The Impact of Non-Cognitive Skills on Outcomes for Young People*. Institute of Education. Available at: https://educationendowmentfoundation.org.uk/public/files/Publications/EEF_Lit_Review_Non-CognitiveSkills.pdf.

19. Gutman and Schoon, *The Impact of Non-Cognitive Skills on Outcomes for Young People*.

20. Francis Green, Samantha Parsons, Alice Sullivan and Richard Wiggins, 2015. 'Dreaming Big: Self-Evaluations, Aspirations, High-Values Social Networks, and the Private-School Earnings Premium', *Centre for Longitudinal Studies Working Paper*, 2015(9).

21. Francis Green, Golo Henseke and Anna Vignoles, 2017. 'Private Schooling and Labour Market Outcomes', *British Educational Research Journal*. Vol 43(1), pp. 7–28.

22. Randall Akee, Emilia Simeonova, E. Jane Costello and William Copeland, 2015. 'How Does Household Income Affect Child Personality Traits and Behaviours', *NBER Working Paper Series*, no. 21562. Available at: http://www.nber.org/papers/w21562.pdf.

23. Gutman and Schoon, *The Impact of Non-Cognitive Skills on Outcomes for Young People*.

24. Ralph Scott and Charlie Cadywould, 2016. *On the Front Foot*, Demos. Available at: https://www.demos.co.uk/project/on-the-front-foot/.

25. Daniel Clay and Andrew Thomas, 2014. *Review of military ethos alternative provision projects: Research Report*, Department for Education. Available at: https://www.gov.uk/government/uploads/system/uploads/attachment_data/file/383304/DFE-RR392_Military_ethos_alternative_provision_projects_review.pdf.

26. Jacoba Urist, 2014. 'What the Marshmallow Test Really Teaches About Self-Control', *The Atlantic*, September 24 2014. Available at: https://www.theatlantic.com/health/archive/2014/09/what-the-marshmallow-test-really-teaches-about-self-control/380673/.

27. Celeste Kidd, Holly Palmeri and Richard Aslin, 2012. 'Rational Snacking: Young Children's Decision-Making on the Marshmallow Task is Moderated by Beliefs about Environmental Reliability', *Cognition*. Vol 126, pp. 109–114.

28. Blanden et al. 'Accounting for Intergenerational Income Persistence: Noncognitive Skills, Ability and Education'.

29. Paul Krugman, 2015. 'The Great Gatsby Curve', *New York Times*. January 15 2012. Available at: https://krugman.blogs.nytimes.com/2012/01/15/the-great-gatsby-curve/?_r=0.

30. Valerie Strauss, 2016. 'The Problem with Teaching "Grit" to Poor Kids? They Already Have It. Here's What They Really Need' *Washington Post*. May 10, 2016. Available at: https://www.washingtonpost.com/news/answer-sheet/wp/2016/05/10/the-problem-with-teaching-grit-to-poor-kids-they-already-have-it-heres-what-they-really-need/?utm_term=.a0f7fc7f535f.

31. Jeffrey Aaron Snyder, 2014. 'Teaching Kids "Grit" is All The Rage. Here's What's Wrong With It.' *New Republic*. May 7 2014. Available at: https://newrepublic.com/article/117615/problem-grit-kipp-and-character-based-education.

32. 'About the Jubilee Centre', Jubilee Centre for Character and Virtues, accessed March 28 2017, http://www.jubileecentre.ac.uk/355/about.

33. Birdwell et al., *Character Nation*.

34. Martin Robinson, 2016. 'The Banality of Character Education', accessed March 28 2017, https://martinrobborobinson.wordpress.com/2016/06/10/the-banality-of-character-education/.

CONSENT AND PUBLIC SPENDING

Exploring new models of taxation

Andrew Harrop

After the financial crisis, when tax revenues collapsed and public deficits soared, social democrats sought new ways of pursuing social justice which were less reliant on public spending. They rightly focused on the reform of markets, on tax justice and on expanding collectivist, non-market spaces outside the confines of the state. Meanwhile, the left's debates on public spending centred only on questions of preservation: where should the previous path of expenditure growth be defended, in the face of a presumption of cuts, or of spending increases far below the trend rate of economic growth?

This turn away from public spending was understandable, but social democrats now have to stop being defensive about expenditure. Other strategies for social justice are still important, but to achieve stronger, fairer societies we need public expenditure to be sustained as a share of national economic output, and to rise in some instances. The case was well made by the 2013 Fabian Society commission on future spending choices.[1] It accepted the need for efficiency savings and deficit reduction, but it also looked ahead over a 15 or 20 year timeframe to examine options for spending as a share of national income. It made two points about the evolution of public spending in the UK, both of which apply equally to other rich nations.

First, spending on health and care needs to rise as a share of national income, in response to cost pressures, demographics and public preferences. If this expansion does not take place through extra public expenditure, it will happen via private spending in a manner which will be more arbitrary, expensive and socially inequitable.

Second, social security policies are leading to a steady reduction in the share of national income redistributed to children and adults of working age. This will result in the living standards of households in the bottom half of the income distribution rising less quickly than those of people who are better off.

Subsequent Fabian research has illustrated this second point in more detail.[2] Current plans for UK social security will see spending on non-pensioners fall sharply as a share of GDP, which will in turn lead to long term stagnation in living standards, greater income inequality and rising child poverty. Higher minimum wages, full employment and tax reforms are insufficient to counter these effects. They can only be avoided by reforming social security policies, so that the default is for spending to rise at about the same pace as national prosperity.

PUBLIC CONSENT FOR EXTRA SPENDING

But if social justice necessitates spending more on both health and social security than current policy assumes, the strategic challenge for the left is to win public acceptance for these increases. Stagnant living standards, political alienation and a more individualistic culture present a hostile attitudinal backdrop. As a result, people will be less and less likely to accept the case for tax rises, unless there are much stronger institutional links between revenue and expenditure. The answer is for social democrats to call for the greater use and higher visibility of earmarked taxes and contribution based entitlements.

Earmarked (or hypothecated) taxes can secure public acceptance for extra revenue raising, in cases where the associated government expenditure is highly valued. They create a link between (unpopular) payments and (popular) public provision, at a population-wide level.[3] Contributory entitlements perform the same function, working at the level of each individual. This makes sense where there is a need to establish the case for the expenditure, rather than the associated revenue alone: earned entitlements linked to a contribution generate public support for spending on things which might be treated with suspicion otherwise.

In the UK context, spending on health and care is popular, but spending on social security for children and working age adults is not. So the former should be the top candidate for earmarked taxation and the latter should be the priority for extra contributory entitlements.

HEALTH TAXES

16 years ago a different Fabian Society commission examined the case for a hypothecated tax for the NHS. The commission's majority supported the proposal, but there was a dissenting minority.[4] At that time, and perhaps reflecting this split, the group's work resulted in a halfway house: an earmarked rise in national insurance for the health service, but not the creation of fully hypothecated NHS revenue. Now there are good reasons to revive the idea of earmarked, ringfenced health taxes - although these days most observers would wish any fund to cover the interdependent fields of healthcare, adult social care and public health.

First, earmarked 'health taxes' would result in spending on health rising automatically in line with tax revenues, which should in turn be reasonably reflective of the nation's increasing prosperity. Linking health spending to a (growing) tax base would therefore combine revenue buoyancy with affordability for taxpayers. There is always some uncertainty in predicting tax revenues, so the income would have to smoothed out a bit from year to year, but a significant top-up from other funds would only be needed in the most exceptional cases, such as the collapse in tax revenues after the 2007/2008 crisis.

Second, health taxes would provide a mechanism for raising extra cash beyond what would arise from ordinary growth in revenues. Health spending could be increased by raising the rates of the associated taxes (thus preventing the crowding out of other desirable public expenditure). Following a process of public education and consent building, a future chancellor might raise the tax rates to resolve existing underspending, for example with respect of adult social care or mental health, or to make gradual, staged increases to reflect rising need over time.

The exact design of new 'health taxes' would be subject to debate, as would the arrangements with respect to Scotland, Wales and Northern Ireland. To secure a broad, buoyant and progressive tax base, the best option would probably be to use a portion of income tax, either on its own or in combination with VAT. Existing 'sin' taxes on tobacco and alcohol could also be used, although they would reflect a small share of the total fund. And the existing NHS element to national insurance contributions (NICs) could be scrapped and rolled into the new system.

New health taxes should be designed to be visible. They would appear on payslips and till receipts alongside income tax and VAT. As an illustration, a set of health taxes that would roughly match existing health spending could comprise: all tobacco and alcohol duties; the first 10 per cent of VAT; the first 10 pence in the pound of basic rate income tax; and the first 20 pence of higher rate income tax. Such standalone taxation for health would be very controversial within the Treasury, but this plan is unremarkable when compared to other European countries, where healthcare is often funded by social insurance or local taxes. And it could be compatible with either a nationally controlled or a more devolved health and care system.

CONTRIBUTORY ENTITLEMENTS DURING WORKING LIFE

Creating standalone health taxes would also serve to increase the simplicity and transparency of national insurance, which mainly funds social security but today makes a small contribution to the NHS too. In future NICs should be explicitly restricted to the financing of contributory entitlements, and this should be clearly communicated to the public to help relegitimise social security. One option, discussed in the recent Fabian report, *For Us All*, would be to convert the existing National Insurance Fund into a ringfenced membership based scheme which would issue regular statements to contributors and recipients.[5]

Increasing the connection between NICs and entitlements should be part of a broader strategy to rehabilitate social security for children and working age adults, by creating a system that provides support to more people, on a more inclusive basis, and therefore secures more public backing. As things stand, the vast majority of the National Insurance Fund is spent on the state pension. Social democrats should develop plans to expand the national insurance entitlements available in working life.

In *For Us All*, three directions for new entitlements are proposed. First, existing support for temporary periods without work – for maternity, unemployment and illness - could be made much more generous. The report argues that earned, non-means-tested national insurance benefits should be set to match the new state pension, which is worth around twice as much as contributory jobseeker's allowance today.

The second idea is that people should have much more flexibility in accessing the lifetime national insurance entitlements they build up. Once people have a good contribution record, they should be able to take a year of their state pension early in order to take time out of work to care or study. The *quid pro quo* would be drawing the rest of their pension one year later.

The third and most novel proposal is to turn the contributory system into a regime for investing in people, as well as insuring them. *For Us All* suggests that funding for post-19 education could work like the state pension in reverse. People would draw down funding to pay for university or technical education. The money would begin as a debt, but would be gradually written off as people make national insurance contributions over their working lives, so that anyone

living in the UK for most of their adult life would end up receiv-
ing a free education. This plan would start to transform the historic
post-1945 model of social 'security' into a system that would also
offer social 'investment' on an open, demand led but contribution
dependent basis.

SOCIAL INSURANCE VERSUS PRIVATE CONTRIBUTION

One of the main reasons why this third reform is attractive is
because of the glaring inadequacies of the the post-2012 debt based
system of student funding in England. When university repayments
are taken into account, middle income graduates can now expect a
marginal tax rate of 41 pence in the pound, stretching over 30 years,
and even then most will still not repay all their debt. Tuition loans
are testing the concept of individualised, account based contribution
to destruction. The new system is proving that public provision that
is as costly as higher education simply cannot be recouped on a fair
basis through personal repayments. national insurance offers a collectivist, affordable alternative.

This is just one example of where social insurance trumps personal account models that do not allow for redistribution or risk
pooling. It is also the case when it comes to insurance for loss of
work, which rightwing commentators often say should be privatised
in one way or another. When you look into the numbers, however,
no scheme without redistributive risk pooling can be designed that
provides low and middle earners with affordable income protection.

This is not to say there should be no place for private sector
welfare institutions. There is a case for employers to provide more
protection and support for their employees, on either a compulsory
or incentivised basis; decent maternity pay is a case in point. And
the new system for second pensions based on personal accounts
is bedding in well. It is opt-out for employees but compulsory for
employers, and based on a tripartite deal where individual, employer

and government all contribute. *For Us All* suggests that a similar scheme could be introduced to help people save their first thousand pounds. But private pensions only work to provide a decent income for everyone in retirement because they sit alongside a strong, contribution based, state pension. It is exactly the same in the USA, which is certainly not the home of the 'small state' when it comes to supporting older people. Private schemes can only be a supplement to state support and never a substitute.

NATIONAL INSURANCE, SECURITY AND INVESTMENT

In the UK, national insurance will always be firstly a vehicle for funding the state pension. But by providing investment early in adulthood, for those who wish to take up the opportunity, it presents an affordable and publicly acceptable middle way between tax funded and debt funded education. And by providing people with meaningful, earned entitlements during working life it can help relegitimise public spending on social security. This is not to say that contributory entitlements should provide that bulk of support to non-pensioners. Any affordable and equitable social security system needs to have means tested and universal components too. But a generous and visible tier of earned entitlement can create more confidence in the system overall, creating the conditions in which future governments can make all the tiers of social security for children and working age households more generous and ensure that spending can rise in line with British living standards.

NOTES

1. The Fabian Commission on Future Spending Choices, 2013. *2030 Vision: the final report of the Fabian Commission on Future Spending Choices.* London: Fabian Society.

2. Andrew Harrop, 2016. *For Us All: redesigning social security, for the 2020s* (London: Fabian Society, 2016); Andrew Harrop, 2015. *The Greatest Divide.* London: Fabian Society; Harrop, Andrew and Reed, Howard, *Inequality 2030.* London: Fabian Society.

3. Andrew Harrop, 2015. "Something for something," in Srblin, Daisy-Rose (ed), *Tax for our Times: how the left can reinvent taxation.* London: Fabian Society.

4. The Fabian Commission on Taxation and Citizenship, 2000. *Paying for Progress: A new politics of tax.* London: Fabian Society.

5. Harrop, *For Us All.*

THE POLITICS OF PUBLIC SPENDING

Ben Page

Over the last 30 years, Ipsos Mori has worked extensively for government and the public sector examining public expectations on public spending and public services.

Despite changing service expectations in response to technological development, more diverse societies, a less deferential society, more transparency and rises in living standards, there remains a strong attachment to universal provision of public services, particularly health services, and basic welfare.

Strong sense of fairness

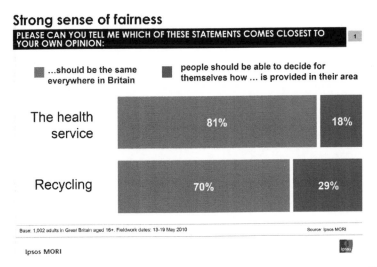

PLEASE CAN YOU TELL ME WHICH OF THESE STATEMENTS COMES CLOSEST TO YOUR OWN OPINION:

■ ...should be the same everywhere in Britain

■ people should be able to decide for themselves how ... is provided in their area

The health service: 81% / 18%

Recycling: 70% / 29%

Base: 1,002 adults in Great Britain aged 16+. Fieldwork dates: 13-19 May 2010   Source: Ipsos MORI

Ipsos MORI

There is continued anxiety about 'postcode lotteries' – the majority of the public does not want to see some health services only available in certain parts of the country, for example, preferring to ensure that they are either available everywhere, or not at all.

In Britain and many other countries there is a schizophrenic view where the majority of the public want both 'more local control' of public services, but also, in the interest of perceived fairness, service standards to be the same across the country.

Second there is considerable confusion about how much governments spend on what services, and of spending priorities. For example, looking at what people in Britain *think* has happened in terms of cuts, is very different from what has actually happened, as our 2015 study showed.

Third, austerity has produced some interesting changes – and sometimes unexpected stability – in terms of public perceptions of the quality of services.

Overall, despite large cuts, particularly in local government services, public satisfaction has held up much more than many would have expected in 2010. Road maintenance has taken a hit,

Public perception of cuts vs reality

I WOULD NOW LIKE YOU TO THINK ABOUT PUBLIC SPENDING ON DIFFERENT SERVICES OVER THE LAST FIVE YEARS. FOR EACH OF THE FOLLOWING, PLEASE TELL ME BY WHAT PERCENT YOU THINK SPENDING HAS INCREASED OR DECREASED IN REAL TERMS OVER THE LAST FIVE YEARS? PLEASE GIVE YOUR BEST ESTIMATE IF YOU ARE NOT SURE.

		Gap
Foreign aid [Foreign economic aid]	Perceived 11% Actual 65%	-54%
Housing [housing development: local authority and other social housing]	-49% Actual -5% Perceived	+44%
Education [all education services from pre-primary to tertiary and others]	1% Perceived -13% Actual	+14%
Pensions and old age benefits [pensions and old age personal social services]	-2% Perceived 13% Actual	-15%
Transport [national and local roads, local public transport, railway and other transport]	0% Perceived -19% Actual	+19%
Other benefits [all social protection not including old age benefits and pensions]	-5% Perceived -1% Actual	-4%
Health services / NHS [includes medical services and research and central and other health services]	-3% Perceived 4% Actual	-7%
Defence [includes military, civil, R&D and other defence and foreign military aid]	-6% Perceived -12% Actual	+6%
Policing [includes immigration and citizenship and other police services]	-9% Perceived -20% Actual	+11%

Base: 1,001 British adults 16+, 8th – 11th August 2015
Actual figures are differences between 2014/15 and 2009/10 public sector expenditure on services by sub-function as reported by the Public Expenditure Statistical Analyses 2015 (2009/10 figures from 2014 publication) and adjusted using GDP deflators given by HM Treasury [figures in brackets are exact definitions]. * Note that education figures for 2014/15 showed a significant decrease due to a decreased impact of student loan impairments, which means the reduction from 2009/10 is larger than the reduction in spending in previous years

Source: Ipsos MORI

Ipsos MORI

with the majority of the public dissatisfied (although even this has declined slightly since 2012) and a large minority of users of care for the elderly have similarly reported a decline, as demand for services rises with an aging population, but local councils find their budgets cut by 35 per cent. But for many services there has been relatively little change. Despite pressures on the NHS, and well-publicised missed targets for treatment, overall patient satisfaction is holding up relatively well – for example, while there are slightly more problems experienced in getting appointments in primary care, the 2015 GPPS survey of all doctors' patients in England shows overall satisfaction with GPs has remained high.

Despite wanting to protect the vulnerable, welfare cuts are generally seen as necessary, although support for them has fallen since 2012.

The public believes 24 per cent of all welfare spending is fraudulently claimed (compared to DWP's own estimate of 0.7 per cent).

What does seem to be happening in the UK is that the public have 'bought' the argument for the need to restrain public spending to reduce the deficit. So even if services have been cut, withdrawn or

Public believe welfare cuts have been necessary

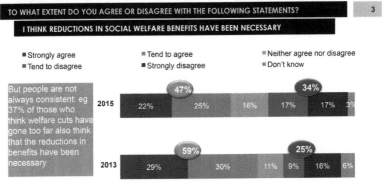

TO WHAT EXTENT DO YOU AGREE OR DISAGREE WITH THE FOLLOWING STATEMENTS?   3

I THINK REDUCTIONS IN SOCIAL WELFARE BENEFITS HAVE BEEN NECESSARY

■ Strongly agree   ■ Tend to agree   ■ Neither agree nor disagree
■ Tend to disagree   ■ Strongly disagree   ■ Don't know

But people are not always consistent: eg 37% of those who think welfare cuts have gone too far also think that the reductions in benefits have been necessary

2015: 47% — 22% | 25% | 16% | 34% — 17% | 17% | 3%

2013: 59% — 29% | 30% | 11% | 25% — 9% | 16% | 6%

Base. 1,006 British adults 18+, 11ᵗʰ – 13ᵗʰ September 2015   Source: Ipsos MORI/2013 BBC Bailout Anniversary poll

Most people don't think they are being affected

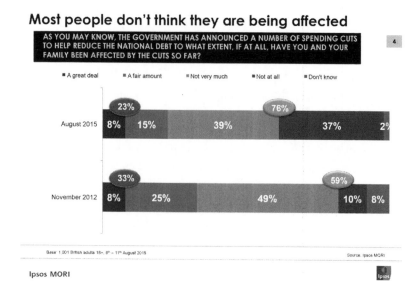

AS YOU MAY KNOW, THE GOVERNMENT HAS ANNOUNCED A NUMBER OF SPENDING CUTS TO HELP REDUCE THE NATIONAL DEBT TO WHAT EXTENT, IF AT ALL, HAVE YOU AND YOUR FAMILY BEEN AFFECTED BY THE CUTS SO FAR?

■ A great deal   ■ A fair amount   ■ Not very much   ■ Not at all   ■ Don't know

August 2015: 23% | 8% | 15% | 39% | 76% | 37% | 2%

November 2012: 33% | 8% | 25% | 49% | 59% | 10% | 8%

Base: 1,001 British adults 18+, 8th – 11th August 2015   Source: Ipsos MORI

Ipsos MORI

entirely reconfigured, there seems to have been some adjustment of expectations. By August 2015 the public assessment was that 28 per cent of necessary savings had so far been achieved. This is far closer to reality than the perception three years earlier in 2012 that 40 per cent of spending cuts had happened.

And when one looks at cuts in spending in general, the public is becoming less, rather than more concerned; only 8 per cent are now very concerned about cuts.

Does this reflect an acceptance that reducing the deficit means accepting less public services? It depends. Looking at local government services, councils have managed to maintain public satisfaction by ruthlessly prioritising on key visible services, efficiency savings and trying to protect services for the vulnerable. There is still real reluctance to countenance any significant council tax rises by the public – and no council has risked a public referendum to introduce rises above 2 per cent per annum.

When we come to the most vital service of all to the public – the NHS – views are mixed about how to meet the funding shortfall. But

No consensus on solutions

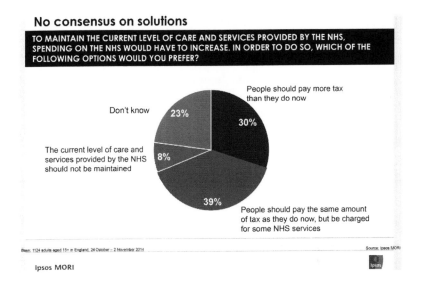

TO MAINTAIN THE CURRENT LEVEL OF CARE AND SERVICES PROVIDED BY THE NHS, SPENDING ON THE NHS WOULD HAVE TO INCREASE. IN ORDER TO DO SO, WHICH OF THE FOLLOWING OPTIONS WOULD YOU PREFER?

Don't know **23%**

People should pay more tax than they do now **30%**

The current level of care and services provided by the NHS should not be maintained **8%**

People should pay the same amount of tax as they do now, but be charged for some NHS services **39%**

Base: 1124 adults aged 15+ in England, 24 October – 2 November 2014

Source: Ipsos MORI

Ipsos MORI

only a minority say they favour tax rises: the rest want to see more efficiencies or user charges, and one in four are stumped.

The bottom line is that there is no easy consensus on how to fund public services in future. Instead, government muddles through and so does the public. In my 30 years of looking at public attitudes on the subject, there may be a tipping point in service levels when suddenly opinion changes and where demand for increased spending – funded, if necessary, through hypothecated taxes or charges at point of use – becomes very clear. But we are not there yet. We still want Swedish services for American levels of taxation, but seem more flexible in our expectations than many in the public sector believed in 2010.

The challenge, of course, is that having done the more straight-forward cuts, we are now facing harder and harder choices, in an uncertain fiscal environment. But public attitudes suggest leadership is possible – while belief in services like the NHS (universal and free at the point of use) remain unchanged, the public are more flexible than we might expect.

CONCLUSION

Emma Kinloch

INTRODUCTION

The relationship between the citizen and state has evolved even if the mechanisms of engagement have not. This lag has created deep unease and has seen the rise of populism throughout the western world. A lifetime of job security is now a thing of the past, trades union membership is dwindling, parents no longer expect their children to have a better life than their own, and identity or single issue politics now trumps traditional party engagement. These are just some of the socio-economic shifts identified by our contributors. The left is faced with a staggering problem; how do we build a coalition of support when so many of the institutions and certainties of the past that bound us together are fragmenting? If this problem is not solved, the left in the UK and beyond risk continued electoral defeat and quite possibly irrelevance. Ben Page identified another impasse in this relationship; namely that citizens' expectations and perceptions of the state and its services are often significantly at odds. This book does not claim to have all the answers but it has gathered ideas that provide the groundwork for a reframing of the debate from the left: working towards a state that is fit for the century it serves and a framework for an engaged and educated citizenry.

INSTITUTIONS AND PERCEPTIONS

This volume recognises that we have moved past the 20th-century Fordism and into a more individualistic and technologically driven 21st century. The old institutions that provided a one-size-fits-all service to citizens no longer chimes with today's heightened expectations of personalisation. Many elements of the solution have been articulated, such as the clear logic of using behavioural insights to retain the dual responsibility the state has to service users and tax-payers, and earmarked taxation for health spending, with a complementary strengthening of contribution based social security. These ideas offer practical solutions to a problem that can often appear insurmountable for the left.

Geoff Mulgan argues that a redefined relationship with the state requires a bigger role for evidence and data. This has been put into practice by the government's Behavioural Insights Team, and our volume is acutely enhanced by Tiina Likki's first-hand experience of this work. However, although behavioural insights give empirical data and evidence that can show policy success or failure they do not take into account the public's perception of the state's behaviour. Ipsos MORI data shows that the public believe 24 per cent of all welfare spending is fraudulently claimed, whereas the Department for Work and Pensions (DWP) believe this figure to be around 0.7 per cent. Charlie Cadywould further underlined this in his chapter in reference to the reintroduction of the grammar school agenda in England. Grammar schools have time and again been shown not to be drivers of social mobility. Nevertheless, when Theresa May walked into Downing Street to give her first statement as Prime Minister she said:

> "If you're a white, working-class boy, you're less likely than anybody else in Britain to go to university.
>
>   If you're at a state school, you're less likely to reach the top professions than if you're educated privately."[1]

This speech foreshadowed her reintroduction of grammars. It does not matter that they are unequivocally not a vehicle for social mobility; it is enough for this Government to be *seen* tackling the social injustice which is evident in society. The inequitable outcomes will undoubtedly be lost in the malaise of Brexit negotiations allowing the right to claim the narrative of social justice which the left instinctively feels is theirs.

This stark gap between reality and perception shows just what a mammoth task faces any state service innovation, particularly any innovations which involve spending commitments. This is of principal concern for the left. The legacy of the 2008 financial crisis has been to appropriate blame to the left for gross financial mismanagement and a rapidly increasing deficit. We on the left know that this was not the full picture, if at all, and the Labour government's world leading role in the wake of the collapse of Lehman Brothers undoubtedly mitigated the effects of the financial downturn. Yet now more than ever we live in a post-truth world where facts are open to debate and perception is king. The simple fact is that the left in Britain is still not trusted on the economy, so a policy platform which advocates, or gives the perception of advocating, a substantial rise in spending will be seen as a continuation of the tax and spend label that the left in many countries finds hard to shift. The policy solutions may be the right ones but the left does not have the political capital to spend. Creative thinking is needed to present ideas to the public that make them feel that their stake in the political process has changed to a more meaningful one. Aside from a lack of trust in the left from the electorate, any ideas which could reformulate the citizen/state relationship are next to worthless unless they feed into the reality of the political process.

CITIZENS AND COLLECTIVE ACTION

The post-1945 settlement gave us the United Nations, Nato and what we now know as the European Union. The paternalistic, collective and comforting nature of these institutions gave a sense of economic, social and political leadership at a time where the

world's deep divisions were laid bare. However, in recent decades
these institutions have had their work held up to a higher scrutiny
through a greater drive for transparency, in no small part demanded
by the proliferation of global internet access. This has heightened
expectations and demystified their work. Transparency has shown
their limitations and made clear that the one-size-fits-all provision
is not a service which serves its constituents. As Georgia Gould
identified, the left has formed its electoral success in appealing to
collective identities; trades unions, religion, class ties and the solidarity of shared experience that those ties historically formed. The
move towards individuality and identity politics has broken these
electoral bonds. It is no longer good enough for the left to rely on
the support of a working and middle class that no longer exists in the
way it did even 50 years ago. Florence Sutcliffe-Braithwaite's chapter noted "being a white-collar worker may not mean what it once
did". The lines on which 'middle class' was drawn in the mid-20th
century have been blurred and the gig economy of the 21st century
has further eroded what it means to be middle class and working
class in this country. University is no longer a guarantee of a gradu-
ate level career and vocational training is treated as a poor relation
in terms of funding and status. The left now then needs to appeal to
a disparate group of people with no strong collective identity. As
Florence Sutcliffe-Braithwaite suggests, one way to cut through the
national picture to focus on localism and devolution. This appears to
be a strategically sound aim. The collective ties that bind us locally:
schools, hospitals, social care, for example, have a tangible cause at
their heart that can be easily identified in local communities. Local
causes and forms of deliberative local democracy such as citizens
assemblies create engaged and educated populations. The renewal of
localism could provide a solid basis for putting our beliefs into practice. Nevertheless, this must only be one strand of the left's solution.
An ever inward looking politics that does not extend further than
our own backyard is not one of our internationalist tradition. This is
a particularly pertinent issue in the wake of the Brexit referendum
result and the looming spectre of a second Scottish independence

vote. Many areas that would traditionally have been described as 'Labour heartlands' resoundingly rejected the internationalism the left has at its core. The 'ever closer Union' was rejected by the British people. The need for a bespoke settlement for the UK is now clear, but the partisan posturing from both the domestic and European political elite does little to counter the disdain of that same group that prompted the rejection of the EU. Chapters in this volume have provided us with options for new forms of collective action where citizens can have meaningful interactions with wider society. The current lack of meaningful relations has indeed led to a lack of service provision that is particularly evident when looking at the experiences of the young.

This collection of essays offers ideas that the left can grow to create a citizenry that is active and questioning but well served by a state that is designed to meet the needs of life in the 21st century. This means that the apparatus of the party political process must also adapt to a new reality where facts are not trusted and traditional constituencies of support can no longer be taken as a given. The left needs to move on from past missteps and offer a genuine alternative to citizens who expect more from them than ever before.

NOTE

1. T. May, *Statement from the New Prime Minister Theresa May*, https://www.gov.uk/government/speeches/statement-from-the-new-prime-minister-theresa-may, 13/07/16.